SLOVAKIA

225 colour photographs
History and sights to see
Countryside and poii
Regional m

MARTIN SLOBODA

INTRODUCTION

S lovakia was at one time a country on our door step that seemed as remote as the North Pole. Today, the youngest Republic within the European Union, and reputedly the 'best kept secret', has excellent air connections into Bratislava. Now lovers of nature, culture and year-round outdoor pursuits can rejoice in this exciting destination. You will discover a sparsely populated country of just over five million people. So the roads are not jammed with traffic, even the cities and towns are easy to drive around. Better still, Slovakia has an excellent railway system. The Intercity Express runs on time, the carriages offer a high degree of comfort and there is first class food in the dining car.

Slovakia is a country that promotes good health in air that is clear and pure. Where you can touch heaven on the peaks of the High Tatra mountains, or explore the hidden depths of the Demänovská ice cave. Do you relish the sensation of soft spongy turf under your feet and the sight of fields of wild flowers? Thrill to the sound of cool mountain waterfalls and the vision of lakes of clear water where you can cup your hands and scoop a refreshing drink? Enjoy glimpses of wildlife like lynx, brown bear and the profusion of birds in the forests? This green and pleasant land in the summer is for you.

The winter sports enthusiast will find ski slopes comparable to anywhere in the world. There are cross-country routes, husky safaris, ski jumps and ice skating. Indeed, Slovakia really is a country for all seasons. If you want to cure your aching limbs after such an active holiday, spend a couple of days at one of the health resort hotels on Spa Island set on the River Váh at Piešťany.

The Slovak capital of Bratislava is steeped in history. This romantic city on the Danube provides a real cultural delight with its secluded courtyard cafes, jazz theatres and music to suit all tastes. Long ago, Maria Theresa, Queen of Hungary made Bratislava a socially acceptable place to be when she took up residence in the romantic Castle. They say the camera never lies; in the case of Slovakia, that is almost true, as you can see from this wonderful pictorial study.

Max Le Grand
British travel writer and photographer

HISTORICAL OVERVIEW

1st – 4th century
The South-western part of Slovakia forms the northern frontier of the Roman Empire

9th century
The Slavs found their own state – the Great Moravian Empire, Christianisation

4th century BC – 1st century AD Celtic settlements within the territory of Slovakia

5th – 6th century
Tribes cross the territory of Slovakia during the great migration of nations

SLOVAKIA

Slovakia is a small central-European country that became independent in 1993, following the break-up of the former Czechoslovakia into the present-day Czech and Slovak Republics. It is similar in size to Switzerland or Denmark, covering 49,000 sq km. Even though the country lies close to central Europe's large tourist centres – Vienna, Budapest and Prague – it was relatively little known until recently. Nonetheless, with a multitude of natural beauty spots and architectural sites concentrated in one relatively small area, it is certainly one of the most interesting places in Europe. The only thing that Slovakia does not have, given its location in the middle of a continent is a sea. Up to now, it has been mostly visitors from the neighbouring countries who have become familiar with Slovakia's beauty, but it is only a question of time before the country becomes a new destination on the constantly expanding global tourist map.

A population of 5.3 million is another factor that ranks Slovakia among Europe's smaller states. Since 2004 the country has been a member of the European Union. Its fast growing economy is based primarily on the automobile, engineering, steel, petrochemical and electro-technical industries. Still, its greatest potential for growth lies in tourism, for which the conditions in the country are ideal. Slovakia may be a small country, but there are sometimes dramatic differences between its regions, resulting from diverse geological conditions. The south, which covers about one-third of the overall territory, is typically made up of very fertile lowlands

For most people, Slovakia is the country of the High Tatras and other places of natural beauty.

There are not many other European countries with such a rich heritage of folklore.

3

13th century, Towns are established; the construction of castles

1000
The territory of the future Slovakia forms part of the Hungarian Kingdom until 1918

1563-1830
Bratislava is the coronation town of the Hungarian Kingdom

SLOVAKIA

The capital of the Slovak Republic, Bratislava, is a dynamic city situated on the borders with Austria and Hungary. Its position, at one time a constraint on its further development, is an asset in the united Europe.

and almost no forests, and enjoys a warm climate with mild winters and hot summers. Grapes, apricots, peaches, melons and other fruits that need warmth and sun are grown there. Most of the rest of the country, however, is mountainous, with deep forests spreading all over its northern part, where cold winters and only mild summers are the norm.

As you move northwards, the mountains get bigger. And it is Slovakia's highest mountains, the High Tatras, that form one of the country's biggest attractions, and provide the image that peo-

Throughout the year, Slovakia hosts a number of musical and folklore festivals, historical, craft and Christmas markets and other events.

ple from abroad associate with it. The Tatras are characterized by deep valleys and steep rocky peaks. Here is found Slovakia's highest mountain, the 2,655-metre-high Gerlach. This small country's unspoilt countryside is truly its greatest attraction. More than 40 per cent of its territory is covered with dense forests, which are home to animals long missing from other parts of Europe. Slovakia's natural treasures are protected in a total of nine national parks, which, together with other protected areas, cover 23 per cent of the country. Slovakia is also rich in

4

HISTORICAL OVERVIEW

18th century
Golden era during reign of Queen Maria Theresa

Early 19th century
Napoleonic wars

1843
Modern Slovak language codified by Ľudovít Štúr

1918
Czechoslovakia established on the ruins of the Austro-Hungarian Empire

karst landscapes with thousands of kilometres of caves. Although all but 12 of them are closed to the public, in order to preserve them for future generations, the dozen that are open to visitors are some of Europe's most beautiful. Five are listed among UNESCO's World Heritage Sites. Slovakia abounds in mineral and thermal springs, which have been used as curative or resting places from time immemorial. Around many of them, internationally famous spa towns have developed.

Whether historic towns or mighty castles, for, history enthusiasts Slovakia is an undiscovered gem.

The part of Europe that is now Slovakia has always been a place where various nations and cultures have mixed, each of them leaving its mark. After the Celts, the Romans and the Teutons, the territory of today's Slovakia became the home of the Slavs, who were later joined by the Hungarians and the Germans. Between 1000 and 1918, Slovakia's territory was part of the multi-national Hungarian Kingdom, known as Upper Hungary, and then part of Czechoslovakia until 1993, except for a brief period as a separate state during World War Two. The languages in common use were Slovak, German and Hungarian.

Slovakia's greatest attraction is its unspoilt countryside with pristine mountains and dense forests.

The nationalities living here influenced one another and enriched their cultures. The effects can still be seen today, although few Slovaks are actively aware of them. Proof of those influences is found especially in the diversity of architecture in such a small area. Well-preserved medieval towns, idiosyncratic folk architecture, hundreds of castles and chateaux, unique wooden churches – those are all examples of the country's rich cultural heritage, recognized also by UNESCO, and have become a magnet for visitors to Slovakia.

The four chapters of this guidebook characterise the main regions of Slovakia – Bratislava, and western, central and eastern Slovakia. At the start of each chapter there is a brief description of the region and a map of its attractions. The book deals with the most interesting historical towns, castles and chateaux, spas, folk architecture sites and national parks. The boxes are used to indicate local attractions. This book will introduce you to this small but beautiful country and help you get to know it better.

1989
Velvet Revolution topples communist regime

2004
Slovakia joins the European Union

1948
Communists take power

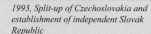

1993, *Split-up of Czechoslovakia and establishment of independent Slovak Republic*

BRATISLAVA

Coronations of kings
Romantic alleys
Musical traditions
L'art de vivre

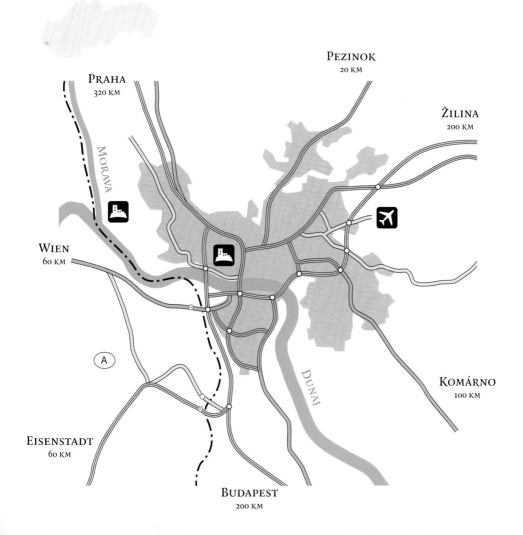

PEZINOK
20 KM

PRAHA
320 KM

ŽILINA
200 KM

MORAVA

WIEN
60 KM

A

KOMÁRNO
100 KM

DUNAJ

EISENSTADT
60 KM

BUDAPEST
200 KM

Bratislava

The capital of Slovakia, Bratislava (population 430,000) is situated in the south-western corner of the country, practically on the borders of two other states – Austria and

of 60,000 students, who are part and parcel of the lively atmosphere of the Old Town streets and squares. Renowned institutions such as the Slovak National Theatre and the Slovak Philharmonic Orchestra, as well as numerous cultural festivals, provide the capital with a rich cultural and artis-

View of the historical centre and the castle from the east.

Hungary. After the split of Czechoslovakia in 1993, the city became the seat of the Slovak parliament, government and president. It is not just the political but also the economic, cultural and scientific centre of the country. Thanks to its strategic location, its excellent infrastructure and highly educated population, Bratislava is now a magnet for foreign investment, helping the Slovak economy grow at an unprecedented rate. As the largest city in the country, Bratislava accounts for 26 per cent of Slovakia's GDP and is the country's motor.

It lies just 60 km from Vienna, and the two cities share not just a rich past but also a very promising future in a new Euro-region. It is already apparent that the region is becoming one of the most dynamic in Europe.

Bratislava is also the seat of three universities with a total

Coronations

St. Martin's Cathedral hosted 19 coronation ceremonies between 1563 and 1830. This glorious era is commemorated by the popular Coronation Ceremony, held every year on the first Saturday in September.

Michalská ulica (Michael's Street) abounds with cafes, shops and galleries.

tic life whose reputation reaches far beyond Slovakia's borders. While Bratislava cannot compete in splendour and size with nearby Vienna and Budapest, locals and foreign visi-

The Main Square is dominated by the Old Town Hall complex.

tors alike appreciate it for its charming narrow little streets, cosy courtyards and many attractions found in the pleasant and compact historical centre, which is a traffic-free zone. In recent years, Bratislava has become a favourite weekend destination for tourists.

The city has grown up along both banks of the river Danube and on the southern slopes of the Small Carpathian mountains. From ancient times, the area has attracted various peoples. Settlements existed here in the times of the Celts, the Romans and the Teutons, as well as the Slavs, who built a Christian church on the castle hill. When the Slavic Great Moravian Empire was conquered in the 10th century, Slovakia's territory became a part of the Hungarian Kingdom. That did not change until 1918, when Slovakia became part of Czechoslovakia, and remained so until 1993, with a brief interval during World War Two.

The first recorded name of today's Bratislava – Brezalaus-

The majestic Bratislava Castle as seen from the bank of the Danube River.

purch, dates back to 907. The name later became Pressburg in German and was used officially, together with the Hungarian name Pozsony, until 1919. That year, a decision was made to change the town's name to Bratislava – a name which probably has its roots in the original Brezalauspurch. In 1291, Bratislava was granted a municipal charter and underwent rapid growth. 1465 saw the foundation of the first university here, named Academia Istropolitana. After the Turks defeated the Hungarian army at the Battle of Mohacs in 1526, they soon began to take over large parts of the Hungarian Kingdom. In front of their advance, all offices in the capital Buda (now Budapest) were, in 1536, moved to Bratislava, which was declared the kingdom's temporary capital. In 1563 the town also became the place where future Hungarian kings were crowned, with the crown jewels already brought here some time previously. Bratislava remained the temporary capital until 1783 and hosted coronations till 1830, while the Hungarian Parliament continued to hold its sessions here until 1848. During this long period, the town was the political and cultural centre of the whole kingdom.

One of Bratislava's characteristic traits, a source of pride for its inhabitants even today, was that it was multilingual and cosmopolitan. Until the mid-19th century, the dominant local nationality was German, but Hungarians, Slovaks and Jews lived here as well. The numbers gradually became even, earning Bratislava the reputation of a trilingual town, which lasted until World War Two. And even though much has been destroyed by the war and the subsequent decades of the communist regime, German and Hungarian are still spoken in Bratislava today, although the official language is Slovak.

For centuries, the 85-metre-high hill over the Danube has

The 85-metre-high St. Martin's Cathedral. View from the castle.

Blue Church

The Art Nouveau St. Elisabeth's Church from 1909-1913, popularly known as the 'Blue Church'. One of the most beautiful sacred buildings in the town.

tion, from a Renaissance fortress to a baroque castle, in order to become the queen's Hungarian summer residence. One of the buildings, erected as an extension to the castle on the side facing the town and called the New Palace, became the seat of the Hungarian governor, Duke Albert of Saxony-Teschen, who became Maria Theresa's son-in-law after marrying her favourite daughter Maria Christina. Albert was a keen art collector and it was here that he started a collection that would become known as the world-famous Albertina of Vienna. However, the queen's residence was moved to Buda in 1783 and later on, while the castle was used by the army, negligence caused a fire in which the castle completely burnt down and was left in ruins for 150 years. It was only rebuilt in the second half of the 20th century.

Below the castle lies the **Old Town**. From the 15th century it was encircled by tall fortifications, some of the western parts of which have been preserved. Entry into the town was effected through three, and later four, gates. The only gate remaining is the northern **St. Michael's Gate**. Its tall baroque roof makes it a landmark of the Old Town.

been the site of the city's and the region's main landmark: a monumental **castle** with four turrets. First the Celts and the Romans, and then later the Slavs, appreciated the hill's strategic position. The castle's history begins in the 13th century. In the 15th century, after King Sigismund of Luxembourg chose it to be his Hungarian seat, the old palace was demolished and the only part remaining, a massive tower, was incorporated in the new Gothic palace that we know today. By the 16th century, the castle no longer met its owners' needs and was rebuilt in the Renaissance style by the architect Pietro Ferrabosco, who also worked on the reconstruction of the Hofburg palace in Vienna. From 1552 to 1783, with some interruptions, the castle's Crown Tower served as the depository for the Hungarian crown jewels. In the 18th century, during the reign of Maria Theresa, the castle underwent a final transforma-

The Good Shepherd's House, situated near St. Martin's Cathedral, is one of the most interesting houses in Bratislava.

The centre of all life in the town is the **Main Square** with the Old Town Hall. Not very

The Opera of the Slovak National Theatre is among the most prominent institutions of its kind in central Europe.

mantic place, with its good acoustics, is the venue for theatre performances, concerts and craftsmen's fairs all the year round.

In the neighbouring Primate's Square is to be seen the largest and the most beautiful palace in the town– the **Primate's Palace**, nowadays a part of the city's town hall. It was built in 1781 as a winter residence for archbishops, and holds a real treasure: a unique six-piece set of English tapestries, which were wovwn for the English king in the 17th century and can be seen in the palace's state rooms. It is the only completely preserved set of English tapestries in the world and was discovered by chance during reconstruction work in 1903. Earlier, in 1805, the so-called Peace of Pressburg was signed in

The grandiose rooms of the Primate's Palace house unique English tapestries from the 17th century.

spacious but cosy, the square could serve as a textbook of architecture. Each building represents a different style and here one finds them all, from Gothic to Art Nouveau. Standing in the middle of the square is Maximilian's Fountain, built in 1572 and now the oldest in Bratislava. The square is the focal point of the Old Town and especially in summer it teems with life; young people are perched on the fountain, while others sit in their favourite cafés or restaurants, enjoying the magical atmosphere of the place. Before Christmas, a traditional market takes place here, attracting tourists from all over Europe with its atmosphere, local specialities and hand-made products. The square is dominated by the Tower of the **Old Town Hall**, originally a Gothic structure with a baroque façade added.

A 15th century Gothic passageway leads you from the square to the beautiful courtyard of the Old Town Hall, with Renaissance arcades evoking a more southern atmosphere. This ro-

the palace, following the Battle of Austerlitz. As the defeated side, Austria lost large parts of its territory to Napoleon, who thereby attained the height of his power. Walking on towards the Danube, you come to another square, a long former promenade, at the end of which the spectacular building of the Slovak National Theatre was erected in 1886. The local opera and ballet performances are well known for their outstanding quality, and Slovak opera singers have become stars of the world's most famous opera houses. An equally famous and attractive building stands nearby: – the Slovak Philharmonic, which is the most elegant concert hall in Bratislava.

Below the castle, and towering over the edge of the Old Town, is the tall silhouette of **St. Martin's Cathedral**, which was completed in the middle of the 15th century and is the largest Gothic monument in the city. A total of 19 Hungarian kings and their wives were crowned here between 1563 and 1830. To commemorate those events, there is a 300-kg

One of Bratislava's landmarks – the recently renovated Carlton Hotel.

In the summer, the streets and squares of Bratislava bustle with life long into the night.

sic are connected with the city, either because they were born here, studied or gave concerts here. Among the best known are Mozart, Beethoven, Haydn, Rubinstein, Hummel, Liszt, Bartók and Dohnányi.

Bratislava's Jews were one of the communities that in the past played an important role in the city's life. The Jewish quarter was located between the castle and the Old Town, and the city had three synagogues. The best-known figure of the community was the Frankfurt-born rabbi Chatam Sofer, one of the greatest scholars of his time, whose advice was sought by people from all over Europe. When he died in 1839, he was buried in an old Jewish cemetery below the castle hill, near the Danube. Only the part of the cemetery with the most

copy of the Hungarian crown mounted on the cathedral's 85-metre tower. In the 18th century, the cathedral's interiors underwent reconstruction in the baroque style, conducted by the Austrian sculptor Georg Rafael Donner, who lived in the town for 11 years. His equestrian statue of St. Martin and the Chapel of St. John the Mendicant have been preserved until the present day.

One of the largest palaces in the city is the **Grassalkovich Palace**, now the official seat of the Slovak president. It was built in the 18th century outside the city's fortifications and belonged to Count Grassalkovich, one of the most influential men in the country. The splendid garden adjacent is open to the public.

In the 18th and 19th centuries, the town had a very busy musical life and that tradition has survived to the present day. When roaming the Old Town's lanes and squares with their many picturesque palaces, you may notice the plaques commemorating the presence of famous composers in Bratislava. Indeed, many personalities from the world of mu-

Bratislava and wine

Winemaking has had a long tradition here. The original wine cellars in the Old Town nowadays house restaurants and bars. Not many people know that, outside of France, Bratislava was the first town to produce sparkling wine by the "methode champenoise" The surrounding hills continue to produce grapes used for making high-quality dry white wines.

Bratislava has a rich musical tradition. In summer, the streets of the town are transformed into musical venues.

Its romantic atmosphere and the traditional Christmas market make Bratislava a popular destination also in winter.

The eighteenth-century Grassalkovich Palace is currently the official residence of the President of the Slovak Republic. The surrounding gardens are open to the public.

valued graves has remained and has recently been turned into the **Chatam Sofer Memorial**, now one of Bratislava's prominent sights.

There are also things worth seeing on the outskirts of the city. In the west, right on the border with Austria, the ancient **Devín castle** towers above the confluence of the Danube and Morava rivers. Set in a beautiful landscape, this large and picturesque ruin occupies a key strategic position. Settlements have existed on the tall, 80-metre castle cliff since ancient times, and Devín is one of Slovakia's most important archaeological sites, full of traces of different nations and civilizations. The Celts settled here and the Romans had an important guardhouse at the castle: the Danube marked the border of their empire and the castle overlooked a strategic ford in the river. Later, the Slavs turned Devín into a large fortified settlement. The current castle was built in the 13th century, on foundations dating back to the ninth. It had many owners and each of them extended it by building a new part. Although the castle withstood a Turkish siege in 1683, it was blown up in 1809 by Napoleon's army. In the period up to 1989, the waterfront just below the castle was a heavily guarded border – the Iron

Curtain separating the East from the West. Nowadays, people from countries all around the world visit the place, where all that remains to remind them of the infamous totalitarian era is a few strands of barbed wire. The castle's uppermost platform offers a magnificent panoramic view of Austria, nearby Vienna and, in good visibility, the Alps. Because of their unique flora and fauna, the hills around Devín are now a nature reserve, but tourists are allowed to walk their numerous paths and enjoy the splendid views of the country.

In the southern part of the city, close to the Hungarian border, stands the **Rusovce Chateau**, built by the Zichy family in the 18th century. In the early 19th century, it underwent a reconstruction in the revival style. At the end of the same century, the famous horse-breeder, Henckel von Donnersmark, bought the chateau and gave it a considerable facelift in the spirit of the English Tudor style. Later, in 1906, he sold the chateau to Count Lónyay, who moved to live here together with his wife Stephanie, Princess of Belgium and Archduchess of Austria. She was the daughter of Leopold II, the King of the Belgians, and came to fame as the wife of the crown prince Rudolf Habsburg, the only son of the

Rusovce Castle

Rusovce Castle lies in a lush park in the southern part of the city. Between 1906 and 1945, it was the home of the Belgian Princess Archduchess Stephanie, the widow of the crown prince Rudolf Habsburg.

Bratislava is a good example for a blend of all kinds of architectural styles.

Emperor Franz Joseph and the Empress Elisabeth. After Rudolf's tragic death by suicide in Mayerling in 1889, Stephanie lived alone for a long time. Only in 1900 did she remarry, taking for her husband Count Lónyay. However, his social status was lower than hers and so all of Stephanie's family turned their backs on her. In 1906 the couple moved into Rusovce and turned the chateau into a prestigious mansion, involving a costly reconstruction of the large surrounding park. They lived here until the end of the Second World War and special guests often came to visit them, including the successor to the throne, Franz Ferdinand d'Este, and the Bulgarian Czar, Ferdinand Coburg. Not far from Rusovce, in the village of **Čunovo**, is a vast reservoir that is the first part of the Gabíkovo water scheme, Slovakia's largest hydroelectric power plant. A new leisure centre is under construction alongside the reservoir which will incorporate the current white-water racing channel, one of the largest of its kind in Europe. European and world championships regularly take place here and the white-water course is also Bratislava's rafting centre. Art has its place in Čunovo too, in the form of the Danubiana Muelensteen Art Museum, standing on a nearby peninsula in the Danube. The imaginative and colourful ship-like building, surrounded by numerous sculptures, proclaims it to be a gallery of modern art. It is one of the capital's newest and most interesting attractions, regularly hosting exhibitions by renowned artists from all around the world.

The massive Devín Castle rises above the Danube in the western part of the town.

Western Slovakia

Splendid wines
Hot springs
Monumental castles
Fertile lowlands

CZ

Trenčianske Teplice

Trenčín

Trenčín Castle

Beckov

Skalica

Piešťany

Smolenice   Dolná Krupá

Topoľčianky

Červený Kameň   Trnava

Pezinok   Nitra

Bratislava

A

H

 Komárno

Western Slovakia

Pezinok

Located just 20 km northeast of Bratislava, Pezinok (population 22,000) is one of Slovakia's winemaking centres. The town lies on the so-called Small Carpathian Wine Route, stretching some 60 km from Bratislava to Smolenice Castle. It connects all the important small towns and villages on the southern slopes of the Small Carpathians where winegrowing has been a long-established tradition. Pezinok was granted its municipal charter in 1376, and in 1647 it became a free royal town. Apart from wine production, mining was an important industry here until the 18th century, gold being the miners' chief object., The town's fortifications, dating from the first half of the 17th century, have been preserved in some places. In the centre, you will find typical wine-makers' houses with large drive-through gates and long courtyards. It goes without saying that each house has a wine cellar. The upper part of the town is dominated by a small chateau with a large English park, originally a wa-

The massive antique barrels in the wine cellar of the chateau once owned by the mighty Pálffy family.

ter fortress built in the 13th century. It underwent numerous reconstructions and between the 17th and 20th centuries was owned by the Pálffy family. Its wine cellar is one of the largest in Slovakia and contains many ancient barrels of gigantic proportions. Upstairs, in the chateau's grand hall, interesting wall paintings are on display. Opposite the chateau stands the most significant ecclesiastical building in the town, the parish church dating from the mid 14th century, with a unique marble pulpit from 1573. Another very inter-

The Town Hall with turrets and arcaded courtyard from around 1600 is one of Pezinok's most significant buildings.

The winemaking traditions of Pezinok

Throughout the year, the town hosts a number of traditional festivals and events like the Exhibition of Wine in April, the Grape Harvest Festival in September, or the Days of Open Cellars in November. The welcoming cellars of local wine producers are open to vintage lovers at any time of the year.

centre, you come across the Schaubmar Mill, a restored water mill, nowadays housing a unique Gallery of Naive Art.

Other winemaking centres in the region are Svätý Jur, Limbach and Modra. Easily accessible, way-marked walking trails and bicycle routes lead from Pezinok through the surrounding vineyards and on to the Small Carpathians, affording wonderful views of the country and the opportunity to make one's way back to Bratislava on foot, along the ridge of the Carpathians.

Červený Kameň Castle

esting building is the Town Hall with small turrets and a cosy arcaded courtyard dating back to the period around 1600. Opposite the Town Hall the current Small Carpathian Museum is a typical example of a 17th century wine

Located in the Small Carpathians, not far from the wine town of Modra and some 30 km from Bratislava, Červený Kameň is one of Slovakia's best-preserved Renaissance castles. In the 13th century it was part of a chain of castles acting as a defence between the Hungarian and Czech kingdoms. In 1528 it became the property of the financier family of Fuggers from Augsburg, who functioned as money-lenders to several Habsburg rulers. The Fuggers were already operating a copper-mining company in Banská Bystrica, and planned to use the castle primarily as a storage place for copper. In a major reconstruction in the 16th century, vast, 70-metre-long and 9-metre-deep cellars were built, but they were never to be used for storing copper, as intended. Instead, it was wine, the typical product of the region, that got to be stored there. During this period, the castle itself was rebuilt as a fortress to defend the region against the Ottomans, with the four massive bastions and multi-storeyed gun-pits with ingeniously contrived ventilation which still dominate the castle. Albrecht Dürer's designs were used to turn the castle into a

Červený Kameň Castle, boasting the largest cellars in central Europe, is one of the best-preserved castles in Slovakia.

merchant's house. Here you will learn everything about the rich history of the town and winemaking, as well as see many ancient wine presses exhibited in the museum's yard and cellars. Pezinok is the birthplace of one of the greatest baroque portraitists, Johann Kupecký, who worked in Vienna, Dresden and Nuremburg. The house where he was born is now a small museum. Moving away from the

The Budmerice Manor, originally owned by the Pálffy family, is only a couple of kilometres from Červený Kameň.

perfect fortress which no one even attempted to conquer. In 1583, Mikuláš Pállfy, who became the castle's owner after marrying Mária Fugger, had the fortress remodelled as a prestigious residence. To that end, he invited many artists, predominantly from Italy. The Pállfy family, who remained the owners of the castle until 1945, were keen travellers and collectors, who brought here plenty of valuable items of furniture from all over Europe. Most have

The Pálffy family

In addition to other castles and chateaux in western Slovakia, the Pálffys owned this castle from the end of the 16th century to 1945.

been preserved and are on display in the castle, with each room presenting the lifestyle of the nobility from the 16th to 20th centuries. The magical atmosphere and the amazing views from the castle are complemented by many other attractions, such as displays of birds of prey by the local falconers, and historical games.

The University Church in Trnava, built in 1629-35, is one of the most significant sacred buildings in Slovakia.

Trnava

Trnava (population 70,000) is one the oldest Slovak towns, gaining the privileges of a free royal town as early as 1238. Founded at the crossing-point of important trade routes, it also quickly rose to prominence thanks to the German settlers who were invited to the country by King Béla IV. A large part of Trnava's unique brick fortifications dating back to the 13th century are standing today, as are many medieval burgher houses and a variety of sacred buildings. Following the occupation of Hungary's Buda and Esztergom by the Turks, Trnava became the seat of the archbishop of Esztergom for nearly three centuries (1541-1820). It was the presence of the archbishops that determined the town's

development for a long time and helped it become a seat of learning. From 1635 to 1777, a university with four faculties existed in Trnava, founded by Archbishop Peter

The University Church in Trnava, built in 1629-35, is one of the most significant sacred buildings in Slovakia.

The finest burgher houses are near the Renaissance tower dating from 1574.

Pázmányi. The two first faculties were devoted to theology and philosophy; later, the faculties of law and medicine were established. The university complex is one of the largest historical constructions in the town. It includes the first early-baroque building in Slovakia – the Jesuit church of St. John the Baptist (1629-1635), also called the University Church, designed by Antonio Canevale and built by Pietro Spazzo. It was modelled on the Il Gesú church in Rome. During the Counter-Reformation, the Trnava church was the largest and most valuable building in Slovakia. Its decorations are the work of Italian, Austrian and home-grown masters. Inside, a unique three-storey wooden altar, completed in 1640, takes up the whole of the rear wall of the church. It is one of the most beautiful in Slovakia and features 27 life-sized sculptures. Right next to the church stands the pretty building of the rectorate and opposite are the academies, both from the 18th century.

Another of Trnava's significant monuments is the imposing St. Nicholas' Church, built in the late 14th century. Its two Gothic towers have Renaissance domes, a replacement for the original tops destroyed in a fire. At the request of Archbishop Emmerich Eszterházy, a chapel designed by J. L. Hillebrandt was built at the church in the 18th century. The elongated square near the church, leading to the Klarisky Church and convent, dating from the 13th century, is lined with pretty burgher houses. The main square in Trnava is the Trinity Square, dominated by the Renaissance tower from 1574 and the baroque Column of the Holy Trinity. Also in the square are the Town Hall, originally a Renaissance construction rebuilt in the 18th century, and the oldest theatre in Slovakia, dating back to 1831. Still standing in the nearby streets are attractive burgher houses of Gothic origin.

After the university was moved to Budapest and the town was no longer the archbishops' seat, Trnava decreased in importance, but regained its status of a Slovak centre of learning at the turn of the 18th and 19th centuries. In 1846, Trnava was connected with Bratislava by the first horse-drawn train in the then Hungarian Kingdom, which greatly helped its development. Nowadays, Trnava is once again a university town and one of the largest in the country, with a strong industrial base.

Dolná Krupá

Beethoven's House

Beethoven visited Dolná Krupá a couple of times at the invitation of the Brunswicks. He stayed in a little house next to the manor, which now bears his name.

The village of Dolná Krupá, situated near Trnava, is associated with the name of Ludwig van Beethoven. In the 18th century, the village was owned by the Brunswick family. Between 1793 and 1795, Joseph Brunswick had a big classical-style mansion built here, surrounded by a large English park designed by the famous German landscape architect Heinrich Neblien. At

Dolná Krupá Manor became famous for the visits of Ludwig van Beethoven.

the mansion, a garden pavilion was built, and this was where Beethoven stayed during his visits. Nowadays it is called "Beethoven's House". The famous composer was a family friend of the Brunswicks and he stayed in Dolná Krupá at their invitation several times – in 1800, 1801 and, according to some sources, also in 1806 and 1810. He dedicated two of his works to the granddaughters of Joseph Brunswick, Josephine and Theresa: the 'Hope' opus 32 to the former and the piano sonata in F-major opus 78 to the latter. He also composed his Moonlight Sonata here.

Smolenice Chateau

The original Gothic chateau was built in the 14th century at the foot of the Small Carpathians in western Slovakia to guard a trade route to Bohemia. Over the centuries, it changed hands frequently, until it was acquired by the Pálffy family at the end of the 18th century. In the second half of the 19th century, a complex romantic reconstruction was started, drawing on French and Italian medieval resources, and this continued into the 20th century.

The complex of buildings is dominated by a massive central look-out tower with a beautiful view of the deep forests of the Small Carpathians. All that has remained of the old chateau are the fortifications and several towers. The chateau is surrounded by a beautiful country park which gradually merges into the forests. A stroll around the area can be combined with a visit to the Driny Cave, the only one in the region. Nowadays the chateau, which can be found at the end of the 60-kilometre-long Small Carpathian Wine Route beginning in Bratislava, is used by the Slovak Academy of Sciences as a conference centre. It is open to the general public during the summer holidays, but one can visit the former chateau chapel throughout the rest of the year and taste the Small Carpathian wines, a very pleasant way to end an excursion.

Skalica

In Skalica (population 15,000), a number of architectural monuments can be seen in a relatively small area. Thanks to its position near the Czech and Austrian borders, this was the meeting-point in the past for various cultures from the west and the south and the town became one of the region's significant economic and cultural centres. Trade, the cloth industry and winemaking once played the main roles in the economic life of the town.

The romantic Smolenice Chateau lies in beautiful natural surroundings.

Thanks to its suffering very few negative effects, Skalica provides us now with a well-preserved model of a historical town. The first written records of the town date from the 13th century and in 1372 Skalica became a free royal town. Religious orders began to move here in the 15th century and helped spread culture and education. Although quite a small town, Skalica was home to four monasteries – there were Franciscans, Jesuits, Paulinians and Hospitallers.

The centre of the town is an unusual triangular square. Its dominant feature is the Gothic Parish Church of St.

St George's Rotunda

Situated near the former ramparts on the outskirts of Skalica, St. George's Rotunda, originally a Romanesque building presumably from the late 12th century, is one of the oldest buildings in the town. While its upper part was used for defence, the ground floor was a chapel. Inside there are fragments of Gothic frescoes.
Some sections of the town's 2 km-long ramparts have survived to the present day.

The Art Nouveau building of the Skalica Cultural Centre with mosaics on its façade is one of the most interesting houses in town.

Michael, originally from the 14th century, with an interesting Renaissance tower with an arcade. Most of the rich interior dates back to the 17th and 18th centuries. The altar-piece was painted by the famous baroque painter from Vienna, Franz Anton Maulbertsch. Next to the church stands the 14th century St. Ann's Chapel, one of the oldest monuments in the town. The Gvadányi house, originally Renaissance, later reconstructed in the baroque style, is another interesting building. The Hungarian general-in-chief and poet Jozef Gvadányi lived here. In the square, one can also find one of the most interesting constructions in the town – the Art Nouveau building of the Cultural Centre from 1905, designed by architect Dušan Jurkovič. The marvellous mosaics on the façade were created by the Czech painter Mikoláš Aleš.

Not far from the square are other significant sights, such as the Franciscan Church and monastery from the 15th century, the Jesuit Church and monastery with a college (1693-1725), the Paulinian Church and monastery (1715-1725) and the Hospitallers' Church and monastery (from the mid-18th century). Ska-

The triangular square in Skalica is dominated by the Gothic St. Michael's Church and the nearby St. Ann's Chapel from the 14th century.

lica is known for its rich folklore and winemaking tradition. Vineyards stretch over the surrounding hills, and the so-called huts scattered here and there serve for wine production, storage and tasting. The best way to explore them is by bicycle. Apart from winegrowing, Skalica is also known for its sweet speciality – the 'trdelník', a cake made according to a recipe brought to the town by General Gvadányi's cook from Transylvania at the end of the 18th century.

The 'Crutch-breaker'

At the foot of the bridge there is a large bronze statue of the symbol of Piešťany – the 'crutch-breaker' – under the Latin words Surge et ambula (Stand up and walk) reminding spa guests of the purpose of their visit.

Piešťany

The most famous Slovak spa town, Piešťany (population 30,000) is situated on the river Váh, between the towns of Trnava and Trenčín. It is well-known for the healing properties of its hot springs, with a temperature of 67-69° C, as well as its healing mud, both of which rank among the world's best and most famous. Unlike other famous Slovak spa towns, Piešťany is not located in the mountains but on a plain, in an area with a very pleasant climate. The powerful effects of the hot springs and the thermal sulphuric mud of Piešťany were already well-

The most luxurious hotel in Piešťany, Thermia Palace, was in 1917 the venue for a secret meeting of the German Emperor Wilhelm II, the Austrian Emperor Charles I and the Bulgarian Czar Ferdinand I Coburg – the allies in WW1. It was here that they heard the news that the USA had entered the war.

The town is connected to the Spa Island by one of the most interesting and architecturally valuable bridges in Slovakia, the Colonnade Bridge from 1932, designed by the renowned Slovak architect Emil Belluš.

Piešťany springs

All the springs in Piešťany, used especially for healing rheumatism and motor disorders are located on the so-called 'Spa Island' on the river Váh. The most renowned bath complexes are built directly over the springs of the healing waters issuing from 2000 metres below the surface of the earth.

known in Roman times. The first written record of the town dates from 1113 and the first descriptions of the healing springs from 1545. Initially, spa guests bathed in holes dug in the ground and filled with thermal water, and were provided with very basic accommodation in the houses of local residents. Only at the beginning

the beginning of the 19th century, several spa buildings were constructed, known nowadays as Napoleon's Bathhouse, but the development was slow. Only in 1889 did a fundamental change take place, after the businessman Alexander Winter hired the spa from the Erdödys. Following several years of massive advertising at home and abroad, he succeeded in turning the small-town spa into a world-famous health resort frequented by aristocracy, Indian maharajahs, Arab sheikhs, as well as crowned heads. The spa blossomed in every respect, with new spa buildings, convalescent homes, luxury hotels and villas appearing one after another. In 1898, the statue of the 'Crutch-breaker' became the symbol of the spa. Nowadays, just as in the past, guests from all over the world visit the spa again, and, following extensive reconstruction, the town is trying to revive its days of glory.

Beckov Castle

Between the towns of Piešany and Trenčín, near the Váh, Slovakia's longest river, rises a steep rock 60 metres high with the majestic, well-preserved ruins of Beckov castle. This was built in this strategic location as a border castle, guarding the frontier with the Bohemian Kingdom. In the 14th and 15th centuries it underwent a substantial reconstruction in the Gothic style. In the 16th century, when the country was faced with the threat of the Turkish invasion, the castle

The sprawling ruin of the romantic Beckov Castle built atop a high rock cliff above the river Váh. In the past, the castle was used for guarding the frontier.

of the 18th century, after the already famous spa became the property of the Erdödy family, were the first, initially wooden, spa buildings, constructed. One of the people who underwent treatment in the spa in such primitive conditions was Ludwig van Beethoven, in 1801. At

was rebuilt in the Renaissance style and fortified, which helped it withstand an attempted seizure by the Turks in 1599. The castle was abandoned after being ravaged by fire several times in the 18th century. However, numerous architectural details and the remains of wall paintings have survived centuries of neglect and the effects of weather. Now, following restoration works, the castle is once again a popular destination, offering panoramic views of the Váh valley and the surrounding hills.

The majestic Trenčín Castle towers above the old town quarter.

Trenčín

Trenčín (population 60,000) is one of the few towns in Slovakia that can boast of being a documented settlement stretching back to Roman times. An inscription on the Trenčín castle rock is tangible evidence that a Roman legion once spent a winter here and set up a military camp which became known as Laugaritio. The inscription is the northernmost relic of the Romans' stay in central Europe, commemorating the victory of Emperor Marcus Aurelius over the Quadi in 179 AD. It can be inspected through a glass wall in the reception area of the Art Nouveau Tatra Hotel, which was built right under the castle rock in 1901.

Trenčín as a town gained regional influence only in the 13th century, when the oligarchic Csák family ruled at the castle. They gradually took control of almost the whole territory of today's Slovakia, at the expense of the throne. Although the town had been linked with the events taking place at the castle and with its history from long before, it began writing its own history in 1412, when it became a free royal town with all the accompanying privileges and obligations. Thanks to the influence it enjoyed during the following centuries, the town was the target of numerous raids and attacks, but more or less successfully managed to fend them all off.

Nowadays, Trenčín is an important town of the Považie region, with a magical atmosphere which you can enjoy in its enlarged central square, in the centre of which stands a baroque plague column dedicated to the victims of the epidemic that struck the town in 1710. The

The characteristic building of the synagogue from 1912.

square is surrounded by burgher houses and its dominant features are an early-baroque church and monastery. Originally Jesuit buildings, they have been known since 1773 as the St. Francis Xavier Church and monastery, and represent a unique symbiosis of architecture, sculpture, painting and artistic stucco decoration. The illusionary baroque frescoes in the church interior, created by Christoph Tausch, are some of the most noteworthy in Slovakia. The last of the buildings enclosing the square is the well-preserved Lower Gate of the town fortifications from the 15th century. Behind it lies another smaller square with cafés and restaurants, and a popular water sprite fountain in the middle. The cupola of the adjacent large Art Nouveau synagogue from 1912, designed by Richard Scheibner from Berlin, is an integral part of the town's panorama. Nowadays it is used as an exhibition hall and has a tabernacle at the rear. A long covered staircase, built in 1568, leads from the town to the castle. It provided the defenders of the town with quick access to the walls, close to the 14th century Church of the Birth of Virgin Mary. Together with the unique two-floor Gothic St. Michael's Charnel House from the 15th century, which sheltered an ossuary, and a town vicarage, the church forms a fortified area on the platform under the castle, called Marienberg. A dominant feature of the alley leading down to the town is the very interesting Executioner's House from the 17th century.

Historical centre

The long Mierové námestie (Peace Square) is at the heart of the town's pedestrian zone. The column in the middle of the square commemorates the victims of plague epidemics. The biggest building in the square is the Piarist Church with a fine baroque interior.

Trenčín Castle

One of the largest castles in Slovakia, it was built as a border fort at the western border of Hungary, protecting the Váh valley. In the 11th century there was already a stone castle on the site with a monumental watchtower, which was replaced by the Romanesque Big Tower in the 13th century. The base is formed by Gothic palaces from the 14th and 15th centuries, which were encircled by an elaborate complex of fortifications, protecting the castle's strategic position. In the Renaissance period, the complex was expanded with the addition of a star-shaped gunnery-fortification by Italian constructors. It was thanks to this that the Turks did not succeed in seizing the castle in 1663. The castle served as a residence for one of the most significant oligarchs in the country in the early 14th century - Matthew Csák - who,

An overall view of the castle reveals its huge proportions. Built in the 13th century, the castle's tallest tower is the oldest part of the complex.

at the expense of the royal rulers, seized two-thirds of the territory of present-day Slovakia. The 30-metre-high castle tower offers a beautiful view over the Váh valley and the surrounding mountains. Legend has it that the 80-metre-deep castle well in the lower courtyard became a symbol of an everlasting love between Omar and Fatima. The Turkish merchant Omar was supposed to have dug the well in order to redeem Fatima, who had been taken captive. In reality, the digging of the well in the rocky massif was very difficult and the task took over 40 years to complete, between 1526 and 1570.

The spa, set in beautiful natural surroundings, enjoyed its heyday in the 19th century.

Trenčianske Teplice

Not far from Trenčín lies one of the most famous spa towns in Slovakia - Trenčianske Teplice. The town is set in a deep scenic glen. The local thermal springs

The impressive Hammam bathhouse was built in the oriental style in 1888.

(37-40°C) and mud are used for the treatment of rheumatism and motor-neurone disorders. For centuries, Trenčianske Teplice belonged to the owners of Trenčín castle. The oldest written record of the mineral springs

dates from 1398. The first reference to the place as a spa is from 1580, and the number of spas here gradually grew. From the early 17th century until 1835, the spa was owned by the Illésházy family, who tried to model it on other renowned spas in the monarchy. However, only the Vienna banker Georg Sina, who bought the spa from the Illésházy family, and his successors, was successful. In 1870, the famous spa house 'Sina' was built, and in 1888, under the command of Sina's granddaughter, Iphigenia d'Harcourt, "Hammam", probably the most famous spa house of all, was constructed in the oriental style. This was the family that built up Trenčianske Teplice's reputation in Europe at the end of the 19th century. Many more buildings appeared in the following decades, enriching the image of this pleasant spa town, which has been trying to build on its famous past. Apart from the healing water, the thing that helps spread the town's good reputation is Slovakia's biggest film festival, which is held here every June and features international film stars. Each year, some of them attach a plaque with their names on it on the local Bridge of Fame. A very pleasant and large spa park with neat pathways leading up into the surrounding mountains and offering attractive views of the environs, makes your stay here even more pleasant.

Topoľčianky

One of the most famous chateaux in Slovakia, Topoľčianky, is located in a small village of medieval origin. While it was originally a Renaissance building, its present appearance is the result of construction works undertaken by the Keglevich family, who owned the chateau in the 19th century. All that has remained from the original design is a courtyard with typi-

Hidden in a large park surrounding the chateau is a hunters' lodge built during the Habsburg era.

The chateau received its elegant façade during reconstruction in 1820 – 1840.

cal Renaissance arcades. The chateau's classical facade was built between 1820 and 1840. Emperor Franz Joseph's brother, the Archduke Karl Ludwig, bought the chateau from the Keglevich family in 1890 and turned it into a summer residence of the Habsburg family. The

In the middle of the chateau is a Renaissance courtyard in a remarkable state of preservation.

chateau, with a typical cupola and a colonnade, is situated in a large English park, which gradually merges into the forest. Under the Habsburgs' reign, the hunting ground around the chateau was one of the most famous in the Hungarian Kingdom. Another member of the family, the Archduke Joseph August, was the biggest wine-producer in the region. He owed that reputation to the former owner Count Stephen Keglevich, who planted large vineyards with the help of French experts. The Habsburgs were also keen horse lovers and had a big riding school in Topoľčianky, where they kept a lot of rare

National Stud Farm

Slovakia's best horse breeds come from here. The horse breeding tradition was started by the Habsburgs.

bloodstock. After 1918, the chateau became a state property and it was used as a summer residence by the first Czechoslovak president, Tomáš G. Masaryk. The traditions founded by these two aristocratic families have survived up to the present day. Even now, this hunting ground is one of the best in Slovakia and it is home not only to many kinds of deer and birds of prey, but also, in particular, to the only bison herd in Slovakia. The European bison became extinct in the wild in the 18th century. Nowadays, Topoľčianky is also associated with the

national horse-breeding farm, producing Slovakia's best breeds. Last but not least, the chateau's high reputation is built also on the Chateau Topoľčianky wine company, whose wines are among the country's finest.

Nitra

Nitra (population 87,000) is a town with a truly eventful history, and now one of Slovakia's biggest. It is a centre of the south-western part of the country, with highly- developed industry and a lively student atmosphere, thanks to its two universities.

The symbol of Nitra, the oldest Slovak town, is the castle hill, visible from afar together with its characteristic silhouette of a tower. The river Nitra flows around the hill. As early as 828, prince Pribina, who ruled the Princedom of Nitra, had a Christian church built here, the first in the Slovak territory, and invited the Salzburg, archbishop Adalram to crown him. A bishopric existed here from 880 and in the following centuries Nitra was an important cultural and political centre. It became

Corgoň

The more than -life-size statue of Atlant, popularly called 'Corgoň', supporting one of the corners of a palace in the Upper Town, has become one of Nitra's symbols and the name of the local beer.

which consists of three interconnected churches. The oldest one is a Romanesque church from the 11th century, of which only a part has survived. A little higher up stands the Gothic Upper Church, built between 1333 and 1335, whose interior was reconstructed twice. In the 17th and 18th centuries it was richly decorated with frescoes and pictures by Antonio Galliarti. It is the main part of the cathedral and one of the most precious baroque cathedral interiors in Slovakia. A broad staircase leads from it to the Lower Church, the most recent of the three. It was built in the baroque style between 1622 and 1642 and complements the whole baroque complex. The Episcopal Palace with its courtyard stands next to the cathedral. It was built in the place of an older, Gothic palace between 1732 and 1739. The star-shaped fortifications of the castle complex were completed in 1674, following the seizure and destruction of the town and the castle by Turks in 1663. Below the castle lies the Upper Town, the dominant feature of which is a pleasant little square with the building of the Great Seminary from the 18th century, housing the priceless Diocesan Library. Opposite stands the Small Seminary from the 19th century. An interesting construction is the early 19th century Kluch's Palace, with a big statue of the Giant Atlant at the corner, whose popular name 'Corgoň' gave the name to the Nitra beer. The Lower Town, with an agreeable pedestrian zone leading to a large square with a modern theatre and a town hall from 1880, is Nitra's

View of Nitra Castle with the ramparts and the Upper Town beneath.

a free royal town in 1248. The historical part of the present-day Nitra consists of the castle and the Upper and the Lower Towns. Nitra Castle is one of the most interesting complexes in the country and is made up of the castle cathedral, the Episcopal Palace and fortifications. The most noteworthy part is St. Emeram's Cathedral,

St. Emeram's Cathedral at Nitra Castle consists of three churches. The oldest one is a Romanesque church from the 11th century, of which only a part has survived.

century. Monks from this, the oldest monastery in Slovakia, left the so-called Zobor documents, describing the monastery and its surroundings. The papers date from 1111 to 1113 and are the oldest preserved documents in Slovakia. Nitra also owes its rich winegrowing traditions to the monks.

Komárno

With its strategic position at the confluence of two big rivers – the Danube and the Váh - Komárno (population 38,000) has, since ancient times, been the crossroads of several important trade routes and a strategic location for many powers. No wonder then that the town was built as a fortress, which resisted a Tartar invasion as early as in 1242. The Danube splits the town into two parts, Slovak and Hungarian, with the latter called Komárom. Thanks to its proximity to the border and its mixed population, Komárno has a unique and pleasant atmosphere. It is one of the centres of Slovakia's Hungarian minority and the seat of the Hungarian University.

During the Turkish expansion in the 16th and 17th cen-

Constantine and Methodius

The statues of these men, who in the 9th century spread the Christian religion over the territory of the present Slovakia, are below the castle. Thanks to both missionaries, priests could celebrate masses also in the local Slavic language.

lively centre. The synagogue nearby, tastefully reconstructed in 1911, nowadays hosts exhibitions. One of the dominant structures here is a monumental baroque Piarist church with a monastery, built between 1701 and 1763 and housing valuable late-baroque wall paintings.

Beyond the river, the monumental hill Zobor towers over the town. As the hill rises direct from the plains of southern Slovakia, it is a dominant feature of the region and in good weather it can even be seen from Bratislava. On the Zobor hillside are located the remains of the Benedictine monastery, which originated before 1000 and existed until the 15th

Each of the 45 houses in the Europe Square in Komárno represents one European country.

turies, the most up-to-date expertise was applied in an expensive reconstruction which turned Komárno into the most important fortress in the Hungarian Kingdom for use in the wars against the Turks. The structure consists of three parts. The old fortress, originally from the 12th century, was completed in the 16th century. A new, pentagonal fortress was added between 1663 and 1673, and was connected to the old part by a bridge. A ring of walls and towers, called the Palatine line and built during the Napoleonic wars in the early 19th century, forms the last part. The fortress of Komárno, which was never taken, is the biggest in Central Europe and the public has gradually gained access to it.

The Town Hall in Komárno is situated in the historical part of the town characterised by its narrow lanes and small squares.

In the cosy corners of the square there are a number of shops and cafes.

At the end of the 18th century, Komárno experienced a series of earthquakes that had a serious impact on the town's life. Following extensive damage, a law was adopted that for a long time banned the construction of houses of more than two storeys.

Besides the fortress and the historical part of the town with its attractive streets and squares, Komárno has another, modern attraction: Europe Square, built in an undeveloped location in the town centre. To symbolise its being a trading crossroads of European importance, the square is lined with buildings representing the typical architecture of 45 different European countries. There are the Millennium Fountain, little shops, cafés and many benches, to encourage you to sit and inspect the particular houses. A walk through the old town will lead you to the birthplaces of two famous artists: the Hungarian writer Mór Jókai and the renowned composer Franz Lehár. From an economic perspective, Komárno comes after Bratislava as the second most important port in Slovakia, and both river and sea-going ships are built in the well-known local shipyards. The nearby village of Patince is a noted recreation centre with thermal springs.

CENTRAL SLOVAKIA

Mining towns
Folk architecture
Rich folklore
Beautiful nature

PL

CZ

ŽILINA

RAJECKÉ TEPLICE

ČIČMANY

STREČNO

MALÁ FATRA

ORAVA CASTLE

WESTERN TATRAS

VEĽKÁ FATRA

VLKOLÍNEC

ŠPANIA DOLINA

LOW TATRAS

BOJNICE

KREMNICA

BANSKÁ BYSTRICA

ZVOLEN CHATEAU

BANSKÁ ŠTIAVNICA

SVÄTÝ ANTON

H

Žilina

Žilina (population 87,000) is the centre of north-western Slovakia and one of the biggest Slovak

The two similar towers are Žilina's landmarks.

towns. The first record of Žilina as a town dates from 1312. As with other Slovak towns, Žilina owes its development in the Middle Ages to German colonists. An important event in the town's life was the issuance of the so-called Privilegium pro Slavis by King Louis I of Anjou in 1381, a document allowing the posts in the town council to be divided equally between Slovaks and Germans. A precious trilingual book from the period is extant, the so-called Book of the Town of Žilina, written between 1378 and 1524, which is the oldest legal document in Slovakia. The book includes a record in the Slovakized Czech language from 1451, the oldest of its kind in the Slovak territory. In the 16th and 17th centuries, the town enjoyed economic prosperity and became an important centre of the region. It was at this period that Žilina became the most important centre of the protestant movement in the Hungarian Kingdom. In the 18th century and throughout most of the 19th, the town stagnated and even saw a decrease in the number of inhabitants. New industrial development came when Žilina was linked with the rest of the country by railway in 1871. Up to the present day, industry has played a dominant role in Žilina's economy and continues to thrive.

The heart of Žilina is the large Mariánske Square (100 m by 100 m). Over the centuries, it has retained its original character and it is the only place in Slovakia where arcades on the ground floors of burgher houses have been preserved along the whole perimeter. In the middle of the square stands a baroque pillar from 1738, commemorating the town's re-catholicisation. The dominant feature of the square is a baroque Jesuit Church with two towers, and an adjacent monastery dating from 1754. The most significant building in the square is the Old Town Hall, which was given its present-day form in 1890. The peal mounted on the facade, which plays every hour, is an interesting tourist attraction. Žilina is symbolized by two almost identical towers standing near the square. The taller one belongs to

In the historical centre of Žilina there are many attractive squares and narrow lanes. The mountains are only minutes away from any part of the town.

the Roman Catholic Parish Church of the Holy Trinity; it was built around 1400 as a Gothic church and later reconstructed in the Renaissance style. The nearby lower tow-

Žilina's central square

Forming the heart of the Žilina Old Town quarter is this 100 x 100 m square that has preserved its original character over the centuries. It is Slovakia's only square with arcades around the whole perimeter.

er was built as a Renaissance belfry in 1530. A narrow street, called Farská (Parish Street) leads from the square to the parish staircase built in 1940. The staircase takes you to another impressive square, with a big terrace fountain. The town's main shopping street with its interesting turn of the century buildings, which is also part of the pedestrian zone, leads from here to the railway station. The Franciscan church and monastery without a tower, is a typical construction of the order, was completed in 1730, and has a much-prized interior. Opposite this stands a former synagogue by the famous Berlin architect Peter Behrens, completed in 1934.

One of the most significant historical monuments in the town is the Budatín Chateau, situated near the centre, at the confluence of the rivers Váh and Kysuca. It was built as a sentinel castle in the 13th century and its oldest part is a 20-metre-high monumental round tower from 1323. The castle was expanded in the 16th and 18th centuries but burned down in the middle of the 19th century. The then owners of the castle – the Csáky family – only succeeded in restoring the castle in the late 19th and the early 20th centuries. Nowadays, it houses the mu-

seum of the region with an exhibition dedicated to the tinker's craft, a craft typical of this part of Slovakia but not found elsewhere in Europe.

Žilina's oldest architectural monument is St. Stephen's Church, named after the king of Rudiny, a part of Žilina. This late Romanesque church dates back to the first half of the thirteenth century.. It is surrounded by a stone wall and houses valuable wall paintings from 1260. Another precious ecclesiastical monument is the wooden Roman Catholic St. George's Church, dating from 1582, in the town district of Trnové.

Strečno Castle 🏰

On a high limestone rock above the river Váh stands the majestic ruin of Strečno Castle which, together with the Old Castle opposite, protected the location where the Váh enters the Malá Fatra mountain range, to the east of Žilina. Records of the castle's existence date from as early as the 13th century. The castle changed hands a number of times; its most important owner was Francis Wesselényi, the leader of the anti-Habsburg uprising in the 1760's. His wife, Zsófia Bosnyák, was looked on as a saint, whose body remains in unchanged form up to the present day. As part of a campaign against the rioters, the then ruler Leopold I Habsburg had the

Strečno Castle was built on a mighty rock above the river Váh. It can be seen from far away.

castle blown up, leaving both the upper and lower parts in ruin. Originally, the Lower Castle was used in the main for storage and manufacturing purposes, while the Upper Castle was the residence of the nobility, with a chapel and a treasury. Nowadays, the reconstructed castle is once more open to the public and offers a spectacular view of the Váh meander and the Malá Fatra massif.

The most attractive part of the Malá Fatra mountain range is the deep valley of Vrátna dolina. It is popular for its tranquillity and good hiking possibilities.

Marked trails lead through romantic valleys and meadows up to the summits.

Malá Fatra

Although not very large, the Malá Fatra (Small Fatra) is one of the most diverse mountain ranges in Slovakia. It lies in the north-west of the country, not far from Žilina. Slovakia's longest river, the Váh, meanders through the range, penetrating deep and splitting it into two different parts. In the west, two castles perched on high cliffs above the river guard the valley – the Old Castle and Strečno. The former is long past its prime and has been derelict since the 16th century, but Strečno, although partially destroyed in the 17th century, has been restored and is now open to the public and used by film-makers from all over the world. The Malá Fatra valley is another canyon (the best-known one being the river Dunajec in the Pieniny National Park) where you can travel down the river on a log raft, accompanied by young men dressed in traditional costumes, who not only navigate brilliantly, but also provide a commentary on the castles, sometimes adding a legend and even singing a song or two. In the past, rafts were used to transport timber from the surrounding mountains to towns in the south, and nowadays it is the most pleasant way to enjoy the beauty of the valley.

That part of the Malá Fatra to the north of the river was declared a national park in 1988, on account of its diversity and its rich fauna and flora. The most attractive part is the Vrátna dolina valley, situated within the mountain range and resembling a cauldron in its shape. It is surrounded by mountains rising as high as 1,700 m and you can only enter the valley from the side near the village of Terchová, through a rocky gap just wide enough for a wild mountain torrent and a path. With a bit of imagination, you will recognize human and animal figures in the rocks of the gap. Beyond, a field of green stretches ahead, and its beauty and tranquillity make it a favourite tourist spot. Rocky peaks alternate with rounded grassy hills, and deep forests with vast meadows. The only settlement in the valley is Štefa-

Folklore festivals

In line with the Slovak tradition, the region around the Malá Fatra boasts its own folklore festival. The 'Jánošík Days' festival takes place in the amphitheatre in the village Terchová every year in early August. When the event is on, the village is full of music, singing and costumes.

nová, a village that has kept its original character and is the starting point for hiking trips anywhere in the mountains. There are many way-marked trails winding through the Malá Fatra, the most attractive and most demanding of which lead through deep narrows and gorges with many waterfalls, called Diery (Holes). Some of them climb up to the main crest of the mountain, which in good weather offers a wonderful view of the whole country.

The Vrátna valley is also a popular ski resort, so it attracts numbers of visitors even in winter. A chair lift operates there both in winter and in summer, taking people up to the mountain ridge, be they skiers or hikers. Winter attractions include dog sleigh races, which have many enthusiasts here. Besides its beautiful countryside, the region is also known for its rich folklore and traditions. In the village of Terchová, at the entrance to the national park, a famous folklore festival called 'Jánošík Days' takes place each year in the local amphitheatre in early August. The festival takes its name from the best-known Slovak brigand, Juraj Jánošík, who was born here. Legend has it that he stole from the rich and gave to the poor. However, after many successful robberies, he was finally caught and hanged in 1713.

Right up to the present, many of the people of this beautiful region

engage in activities closely connected with the surrounding countryside. Thanks to an abundant wood supply, the local people traditionally have been keen on carving. Sheep graze in the meadows on the foothills of the mountains, providing milk for various kinds of cheese that have earned the region its good reputation throughout Slovakia.

Rajecké Teplice

O nly a few kilometres south of Žilina and not far from the majestic Lietava castle lies the little spa town of Rajecké Teplice. Five thermal springs were discovered here as early as the 14th century, but they only came

With its 38°C thermal spring, the Rajecké Teplice spa offers excellent opportunities for treatment and relaxation.

The Aphrodite bathhouse is surrounded by a beautiful park with a lake.

into use in the 17th century, during the era of the Thurzo family, the owners of the nearby castle. However, real development did not come until the late 19th and early 20th centuries. The town is set in a beautiful valley surrounded by wooded hills. In recent years, the town has undergone extensive reconstruction which has turned it into one of the most modern in Slovakia. The local thermal springs, with a temperature of 38° C, are used for the treatment of motor and neurone disorders . The most attractive parts of the spa are a house called Aphrodite, modelled on the Roman spas, and a very pleasant park with a lake, where you can take a boat. Rajecké Teplice is becoming a popular spot for tourists, who welcome the chance to relax there after their sightseeing around the region, or hiking or skiing in the mountains.

Čičmany's tourist attractions are the 140 painted wooden houses.

Čičmany

Located in the mountains between Rajecké Teplice and Bojnice, Čičmany is one of the most remarkable villages in Slovakia. Almost 140 wooden houses have been preserved in this small isolated place. What makes them special is that they are all decorated with white ornaments featuring animal and plant motifs, geometric patterns and runes. This is the only place in Slovakia where such decorations can be seen. The ornaments were originally supposed to provide human dwellings with magical protection against forces from the surrounding countryside. The number of houses like this in Čičmany was previously higher, but over a period of time they succumbed to fire and the devastation of war. After major fires in the early 20th century destroyed 75 per cent of the houses, Čičmany was restored almost to its original form by the renowned Slovak architect Dušan

Painted houses

Nowhere else in Slovakia are there similar wooden houses painted with white animal and plant motifs, geometric ornaments and runes. The local inhabitants believed their magic power could save them from the forces of nature.

Jurkovič in 1923. In the past the inhabitants of the village worked mainly in the surrounding forests and raised sheep, but nowadays they are increasingly engaged in tourism. Above the village you will find a developing ski resort.

Čičmany is also renowned for richly decorated costumes.

Apart from its unique architecture, the village is also noted for the richly decorated folk costumes that the locals wear on various festive occasions.

Bojnice

R ecords of the existence of Bojnice Royal Castle, built on a travertine hillside, date back to the early 12th century. After many centuries and many owners, the 19th century saw the castle's reconstruction into a chateau in the romantic style, inspired by chateaux in the Loire valley in France. The story goes that the reconstruction had its origins in the love of the owner, Ján Pálffy, for a French noblewoman, whose father would not let her marry Pálffy unless the living conditions on his estate could compare with what his daughter was used to at home. So, a major reconstruction began in 1889, but neither the count nor his bride-to-be saw its completion, due to Pálffy's death

The Bojnice Chateau bears a resemblance to the chateaux on the river Loire in France.

in 1908. It is claimed that his ghost haunts the chateau's corridors, a tale which was the inspiration for the International Ghosts and Spirits Festival which takes place here each May and offers varied entertainment, such as historical games and scary characters.

The chateau's impressive interiors, reconstructed in the 19th century in the spirit of the Tyrolean Gothic style, include the unique Gothic altar, the work of a prominent 14th-century Florentine painter. It is installed in the chateau's pentagonal tower.

The chateau has a well, which originated from a crater in the hill and is connected to a cave with numerous small lakes, located under the chateau. This best-preserved

The Golden Hall is one of its many superbly decorated interiors.

and most visited chateau in Slovakia is situated in a park which contains other attractions also.

The neighbouring spa, well-known since the 16th century, provides treatment to people suffering from motor disorders. The thermal swimming pool offers not only relaxation and entertainment, but a beautiful view of the chateau as well. Nearby, Slovakia's largest and oldest zoo park attracts crowds of people of all ages.

Kremnica

K remnica (population 7,000) is the smallest of the mining towns in central Slovakia forming the so-called golden triangle. While the others, Banská Bystrica and Banská Štiavnica, are known respectively as the copper and the silver towns, in Kremnica gold was the precious metal extracted. The Kremnica Hills, rising to 1,300 m and surrounding it on all sides, furnish the town with its beautiful setting. Gold was mined here from the 11th century and Kremnica became a free royal town in 1328, following privileges granted by the Hungarian King, Charles Robert of Anjou.

The arrival of 'guests' from Kutná Hora, the then centre of mining and coinage in the Czech Kingdom, contrib-

Dominating Kremnica are the castle and the St. Catherine's Church from the 15th century.

view of the town and surrounding mountains. Most of the sights in Kremnica are concentrated around its large central square. The most striking venues are the Gothic and Renaissance houses, the building of the mint, Gothic in origin, the Gothic town hall, the Špitálsky church from the 14th century and a Franciscan church and monastery from the 17th century. Also in the square, you will find the Museum of Coins and Medals, founded in 1890. In the past, the parish church stood in the middle of the square, but it had to be pulled down in 1880 following an earthquake. However, another structure remains standing - the beautiful, 19 metre baroque Holy Trinity plague column, created by Dionýz Stanetti between 1765 and 1777 and nowa-

uted to the further development of mining and coinage in Kremnica. The mint founded here in 1329 is now the world's oldest operating factory of its kind, making coins and medals for many countries. Between the 14th and 16th centuries, Kremnica ducats were among the most popular tender in Europe.

The most important monument in the town is the castle, dating from the period between the 13th and 15th centuries, located above the town and dominating a wide area. A Romanesque rotunda from the 13th century is the old-

Miners' Houses

In the past, Kremnica was the centre of a gold mining region. In the surroundings of the town, there are a number of typical miners' houses dating back several centuries.

The church tower offers panoramic views of the town and the surrounding hills.

est structure in the castle. The main part of the castle is the Gothic St. Catherine's Church from the 15th century with its priceless interior, while its tower offers a spectacular

days one of the tallest in Slovakia. In the upper part of the square you can see the house where Ján Levoslav Bella, one of the most important Slovak composers from around the turn of the 19th and 20th centuries, lived and worked. Right up to the present day, Kremnica has preserved parts of its 15th century fortifications, including several bastions and the one surviving gate which gives access to the town from the south. To the north of the centre, you can find the Kremnica knocking tower (klopaka) dating from the 18th century, once used to call the miners to work. Around the town, numbers of the typical miners' houses have been preserved. With its thermal swimming pool (fed by springs attaining 52° C), its beautiful countryside, a rich history, as well as excellent conditions for downhill and cross-country skiing in the area, Kremnica is destined to be a centre of tourism all the year round.

Banská Štiavnica

Formerly one of the most important mining towns in Europe, Banská Štiavnica (population 10,800) stretches over the steep slopes of the hills Glanzenberg, Paradiesberg and Frauenberg in the Štiavnica Hills, in the southern part of central Slovakia. It lies directly over what were once rich deposits of silver and gold, which for hundreds of years shaped the face of this hilly region and the lives of its people. As early as the 11th century, a settlement was founded on the top of the hill Glanzenberg, at a location where ore was discovered near the surface. In 1238, King Béla IV granted Banská Štiavnica special privileges and invited miners from Tyrol and Saxony to the town, sparking off rapid growth. The 15th century was Banská Štiavnica's most noteworthy era and then 1627 saw the first use of gunpowder in Europe, which helped the local miners increase production. At the turn of the 17th and 18th centuries, mining in Banská Štiavnica encountered a serious crisis. The complex of shafts had become so extensive and deep (up to 300 m) that the technology of the period was no longer capable of draining the surface water flooding the mines. Imperial Vienna faced the prospect of losing one of its most lucrative

The Calvary

Erected on the Scharfenberg hill in the mideighteenth century, the Calvary is the most significant complex of its kind in Slovakia. It consists of 23 chapels with a number of beautiful paintings and sculptures. The top chapel offers stunning views of the whole town and the surrounding hills.

The abundance of historical buildings in the town centre has earned Banská Štiavnica a place among the UNESCO World Heritage Sites.

production sites. Finally, two ingenious engineers, Matej Kornel Hell and Samuel Mikovíni, designed a unique system comprising several dozen water reservoirs around the area, providing the power to propel the machinery to drain the mines. New mining technologies were also introduced with the help of the town's Mining Academy, set up in Banská Štiavnica by Maria Theresa in 1762 as the world's first technological college. Students came to it from all over Europe and, according to sources from that era, Banská Štiavnica was the liveliest student town east of Heidelberg. The academy served as a model when the Paris Polytechnic School was founded

Built on hillsides, Banská Štiavnica is one of Slovakia's most picturesque towns.

Serving as a fortress in the wars against the Turks, the 16th-century New Chateau dominates the surrounding countryside.

in 1795, and produced nearly 10,000 experts, who went on to work in the world's most prominent mining, metallurgical and forestry institutions and companies. The revenues and fame that Banská Štiavnica gained from mining its precious metal resources made it a town with a unique, compact historical centre, now listed as a UNESCO World Heritage Site, together with the surrounding water reservoirs, called 'tajchy'. The reservoirs are especially popular with visitors to Banská Štiavnica in summer, but are well worth a visit at any time of the year.

The dominant feature in Štiavnica is the Old Chateau. A Romanesque basilica was built here as early as the 13th century,. At the turn of the 15th and 16th centuries it was reconstructed into a Gothic church with a protective wall. Two older Gothic towers from the 14th century, the entrance tower and the tower Himmelreich,, which served as a prison, were also incorporated into the wall.. In the 16th century, at the threat of an imminent Turkish invasion, the church was rebuilt as a fortress. The windows were walled

up, the arches removed, and the main nave turned into the courtyard of the fortress. The latest adjustment came in the 18th century, when the top of the entrance tower was

The 'Klopačka' tower

Financed and built in 1681 by the miners themselves, Klopačka was used for calling miners to work by way of an attendant knocking on a wooden plate. Similar towers were built in most of the mining towns in the country. The ground floor was used as a prison for the miners. Klopačka offers great views of the historical centre and the Old Chateau.

raised by adding a new baroque structure. All that has remained from the original construction is the Romanesque St. Michael's Chapel with a charnel house.

Standing on the Frauenberg hill, opposite the Old Chateau, is the New Chateau, built as a Renaissance fortress against the Turks in the mid-16th century. It is a massive six storey building with circular corner bastions, to which the town's fortifications were linked. At the same time, the chateau was used as an observation point – it was from here that people were alerted to fires by horns being sounded. And that sound can still be heard all over the town in the summer months, telling the time every 15 minutes.

The central Námestie sv. Trojice (Holy Trinity Square) is dominated by the monumental yet elegant plague column with the sculpture of the Holy Trinity, built by Di-

The Old Chateau, a fortified church later converted into a fortress, is another dominant feature of Banská Štiavnica.

onýz Stanetti between 1759 and 1764. Two of the sides of the square are lined with houses once owned by rich townsmen and mining entrepreneurs. Most of them were built in the 16th century and now, after restoration, have their original late-Gothic and Renaissance architecture and painted decorations. One curious feature is that they provided direct access to the tunnels of the mine. Between 1744 and 1751, a calvary was built on the Scharfenberg

The streets are flanked by Gothic and Renaissance houses.

hill below the town. Sensitively set into the area, it is the most important complex of its kind in Slovakia. The particularly fine view from the upper chapel extends not just over the town, but over the surrounding mountains as well. Above the town, on the road to the village of Štiavnické Bane, the miners themselves subscribed to build a „knocking tower" in 1681. From this tower they would be called to work by a person knocking on a wooden board. Thanks to the efforts of students, one of Banská Štiavnica's most impressive traditions has survived to the present day. Called „Salamander", and held in the second week of September every year, it is a pageant in which people in period costumes make a procession through the town, recreating the atmosphere of the town's days of glory. If you want to experience for yourself what it feels like to be in a mine, there are two tunnels you can enter: the Glanzenberg mine dating from the 13th century, leading underneath the town, or the Bartolomej mine from 1698. Visitors to the latter have included Maria Theresa's husband, Francis Stephen of Lorraine, their sons and future emperors Joseph and Leopold, and their prospective brother-in-law, the Duke Albert of Saxony-Teschen.

Svätý Anton

Only 4 km to the south of Banská Štiavnica, on the site of a former medieval castle surrounded by dense forests and a large park, stands a monumental four-wing late-baroque manor called Svätý Anton. It was commissioned by imperial army general and regional governor Andrew Joseph Koháry between 1744 and 1751. The Koháry family, who owned the mansion between 1622 and 1826, belonged to the new aristocracy that became rich thanks to royal gifts, which they received for taking part in the fight against the Turks. After a marriage united the Koháry family with the family of Coburgs in 1816, the mansion and the adjacent property fell into the hands of the latter. Although relatively few in number, by the mid 19th century, the Coburgs had become one of the most influential families in Europe, with representatives at many a royal court on the Old Continent and elsewhere. The last owner of Svätý Anton was to be the Bulgarian Emperor Ferdinand I Coburg, who left his mark on every room of the manor. A keen hunter and nature lover, his trophies now decorate the interiors of the palace, which retain their original furniture. Although it now houses a hunting museum, the manor has been preserved almost completely in its original form. Its architecture was designed to symbolize the stages of

The manor has been preserved in its original shape.

The Chinese Room is one of the most impressive in the manor.

Turkish invasions. The Italian architects Pratoveteri, Pozzo and Speciecasa, who worked in the central Slovak mining towns, took part in the reconstruction. Later, the chateau's importance for the country's defence declined and, following a reconstruction in the baroque style, it served as the seat of the regional government. The most significant parts of the chateau that have been preserved include a late-Gothic chapel, a knights' hall, and a baroque hall with a painted wooden ceiling divided into 78 sections, each with a picture of a Roman emperor or a Hungarian king.

the year: thus, it has 4 gates, 12 chimneys, 52 rooms and 365 windows. The most impressive wing is the northern entrance. The main staircase, inspired by that of the Schönbrunn palace in Vienna, is decorated with stone sculptures in the style of the famous Austrian baroque sculptor George Rafael Donner. From among the many rooms in the mansion, the Main Room, the Imperial Room, the Mirror Room, the Audience Room, the Chinese Room and the Officers' Room stand out as the most remarkable. In the southern wing, there is a chapel with wall paintings by Anton Schmidt. In the nearby classical English park, the festival of the Days of St. Hubert, named after the patron saint of hunters, takes place in September every year.

This hunters' manor was fortified in the 16th century.

Zvolen Chateau

Towering above the historical central Slovak town of Zvolen, the chateau was built in the 14th century, during the reign of Louis I, a Hungarian monarch from the Anjou family. Its design was inspired by Italian castelli of that period. Originally a hunters' chateau, it wasn't originally fortified, and its rooms, including a knights' hall, faced the town. In the 16th century, the chateau belonged to the Thurzos, who were wealthy mining entrepreneurs and had the chateau rebuilt into a Renaissance fortress, incorporating it into a defensive system designed to ward off

Banská Bystrica

Situated in a valley on the river Hron and surrounded by four mountain ranges, Banská Bystrica (population 85,000) is the natural and administrative centre of central Slovakia. Its geographical location makes it one of the most beautiful towns in Slovakia. The riches of the surrounding mountains provided the food for the first set-

Folk art

The villages surrounding Zvolen are noted for their richly decorated costumes and special musical instruments. The most typical traditional musical instrument in Slovakia is 'fujara', a wooden pipe that can be up to two metres long.

Banská Bystrica is surrounded by high mountains.

beautiful in Slovakia, with many of its typical burgher houses well preserved to the present day. The square is the liveliest part of the town, especially in summer, when the outdoor cafes and restaurants are busy with the town's university students and tourists, giving the square the atmosphere of a seaside town. A dominant feature of the square is the Clock Tower, today leaning slightly, built in 1552 in the Renaissance style and partially rebuilt in the 18th century. It is open to the public and offers a panoramic view of the town and the surrounding hills. The Cathedral of Saint Francis Xaverius, dating from the beginning of the 18th century, with its two unusual turrets which were added during its 19th century reconstruction,

tlers of today's Banská Bystrica, who made their living not only by hunting and fishing but also from silver mining. In 1255, the Hungarian King Béla IV granted the town substantial privileges and attracted German settlers who further developed the mining of precious metals, especially copper, in tandem with its original inhabitants. Banská Bystrica's heyday as the centre of copper mining is closely associated with the Thurzo and Fugger families. Thanks to their joint venture founded in 1495, the copper extracted was exported over the whole of Europe and the town experienced a period of prosperity, which was reflected in its architecture. The centrepiece of the town is an irregularly shaped square which, even by medieval standards, was particularly large. This is one of the most

Copper-based prosperity

The façades of many houses are decorated with the coats of arms of families who got rich from copper mining. The Thurzo-Fugger mining company, established in 1495, exported copper all over Europe.

is only a couple of metres away in the corner of the square (Banská Bystrica has been the seat of the bishop since 1776). The Thurzo House, once the seat of the Thurzo-Fugger Company and one of the most beautiful buildings in the centre, with its artistic Renaissance façade decoration, is located on the same side of the square. The Beniczky House on the opposite side of the square features an interesting portal and a Renaissance loggia on its first floor. At the upper end of the square is the Town Citadel, which nowadays no longer has any fortifications, although the original buildings have been preserved. The most precious one is the Church of the Virgin Mary – the so-called "German Church", one of the most beautiful sacred buildings in Slovakia. Originally a Romanesque church from

Some houses from the town's sixteenth-century heyday have been preserved until now.

In the summer, the outdoor cafes quickly fill up.

experimental architecture from the 1960s. The uprising, which began in Banská Bystrica in August 1944, was one of Europe's biggest anti-Nazi movements.

The charming character of this historical town, with its wealth of well-preserved monuments, and the beautiful national parks and numerous ski resorts in its surroundings, makes Banská Bystrica an all-the-year-round centre of tourism.

Špania Dolina

Situated 11 km to the north of Banská Bystrica, Špania Dolina is one of the most picturesque villages

1255, it was reconstructed in the Gothic style in the 14th century and, after a major fire which engulfed the town in 1761, it was finally rebuilt in the baroque style. Miraculously, the late-Gothic altar of St Barbara by Master Pavol of Levoča from 1509 survived in a side-chapel dedicated to St.Barbara, the patron saint of miners. A precious late-Gothic sculpture of Christ on the Mount of Olives can be admired on the outside of the church. The Gothic Matthias House, the so-called "Slovak Church" and the former Town Hall, now a gallery with a fine Renaissance arcade loggia, complete the Town Citadel. Another attraction of Banská Bystrica, the Museum of the Slovak National Uprising, is an interesting demonstration of Slovak

One of Slovakia's most picturesque villages is hidden deep in the mountains.

of central Slovakia. This former mining village lies high in the mountains at the end of a deep valley. Copper was extracted here as early as the 13th century, and by the 16th century it was one of the mining centres of the Thur-

The landmark of the central square is the leaning Clock Tower dating from 1552.

Lace making

Špania Dolina used to be renowned for its lace making. In the 19th century it was the seat of a prominent lace-making school. The tradition has survived until the present, and one can often see local women sitting in the square making laces for sale to tourists.

The village was built on steep mountain slopes.

19th century, a prominent lace-making school was founded here. This tradition has survived up to the present, and in the summer you can see the local women making and selling their lacework on the square. The best way to enjoy Špania Dolina is by walking the pathways around the houses, or over the surrounding slopes and former spoil heaps which offer striking views of the whole area.

Vlkolínec

Vlkolínec is a unique mountain village.

zo-Fugger Company. The former miners' houses, today mostly converted to chalets, stand on terraced slopes around a square which is the only flat area in the village. Almost all of the houses have retained their ventilation shafts and their typical feature, a large wooden balcony. Most of the houses date from the 17th and 18th centuries; however, some of them are more than 500 years old. Dominating the village is the church, originally built in the Romanesque style and then reconstructed in 1593. A covered wooden stairway leads steeply up to the church from the square. A Renaissance 'klopačka' tower from the 16th century, which was used for signalling the start of the miners' working day, is another monument of note. The last remaining part of the wooden aqueduct, dating from the 16th to 18th century, similar to those built in the Alps, which was used for bringing water to power the mining machinery from as far away as 33km, high up in the Low Tatras, is an interesting technological monument. In the past, Špania Dolina was known for its lace making. In the

Vlkolínec is an isolated village situated high up in the mountains on the eastern edge of the Veľká Fatra mountain range, near the town of Ružomberok. It is located in beautiful natural scenery surrounded by high peaks and meadows offering breathtaking views. Vlkolínec is a unique, well-preserved sample of a Car-

Wooden houses

The 45 traditional wooden houses have been preserved thanks to the isolation and inaccessibility of this village on the outskirts of the Veľká Fatra National Park.

pathian mountain village and for that reason it was declared a UNESCO World Heritage Site in 1993. The village numbers 45 wooden houses built on a steep slope and painted in the typical colours – blue, pink or white. Although the village is a reserve of folk architecture, it is not a museum. It is an authentic original mountain settlement typical of Slovakia's past. It was founded as early as the 14th century and it is still inhabited. It makes a great starting-off point for hiking in the Veká Fatra mountains.

Veľká Fatra

The Veľká Fatra National Park is a mountain range in the central part of Slovakia, with the neighbouring Low Tatras on the east. Its highest point is 1600 metres above sea level. The Veľká Fatra stretches from north to south over an area of 45 by 20 kilometres. With the exceptions of small areas on the hilltops, deforested in the 16th century to provide pastures, the entire mountain

Veľká Fatra is remarkable for its long deep valleys with unique flora and fauna.

range with its long and deep valleys is densely wooded. As human settlement has practically been limited to the borders of the national park, the forests have survived in their original state in many areas. Thanks to the remoteness and inaccessibility of a large part of the mountain range, there is an important population of bear and lynx, and the area is rich in flora, including the rare yew-tree. The longest and the largest valley of the park is the Ľubochnianska dolina which runs north from the heart of

Active relaxation

Biking is one of the best ways to explore the valleys of the national park. Hikers can choose from plenty of marked trails leading to the mountaintops.

the national park. The valley begins at the foot of one of the highest mountains and a reasonable 25km trail, ideal for cyclists, winds along the stream at its bottom. The Ski Park Ružomberok ski resort was built near the town of Ružomberok and the well-known village of Vlkolínec on the northern border of the mountain range. Several beautiful valleys with picturesque villages stretch westwards from the main ridge of the mountain range. Another ski resort is situated at the entrance to the Jasenská dolina valley. The Museum of the Slovak Village, with precious examples of folk architecture from all over the country, was established not far away,

Villages surrounding the Veľká Fatra mountain range.

Museum of the Slovak Village

On the outskirts of the town of Martin near Veľká Fatra is the Museum of the Slovak Village. Built up gradually over long decades, the museum exhibits precious examples of folk architecture from throughout Slovakia.

on the outskirts of the town of Martin. A village with representative samples of the different regions of Slovakia has been created in an authentic environment. Traditional gardens, fields, workshops with craft demonstrations, pets and domestic animals, an old pub as well as a number of interesting events throughout the year add to the popularity of this museum with both Slovak and foreign visitors. The most beautiful part of the Veľká Fatra is the area around Blatnica, which has retained its traditional character. It is the starting point for trips to the 18 km long Gaderská dolina valley, a scenic canyon with bizarre limestone and dolomite cliffs. It has a sur-

country skiing attract many tourists to this mountain pass. The surrounding hills are well-known as one of the most suitable areas for paragliding in the country. Renowned for dogsled races, Donovaly has already hosted several European and World Championships in this attractive sport.

Low Tatras 🌲

The Low Tatras are a large mountain range extending across the central part of Slovakia. They form a vast natural barrier, consisting of several different regions and bordered by broad valleys to the north and south. Around 100km long and 20km wide, the Low Tatras stretch from west to east where they merge with other mountain ranges. The Váh and the Hron, the two longest Slovak rivers, both have their sources in the Low Tatras. As a result of the difficult natural terrain, only one road crosses the mountains, and the Čertovica mountain pass on this road has become a popular ski re-

The Low Tatras mountain range with summits up to 2000 m above sea level is the largest natural barrier in central Slovakia.

faced track suitable for bike trips. The southern side of the mountains features a karstic area with several caves. Only one of these – the Harmanecká Cave - is accessible to the public and it is noted for its white dripstones, large stalagmites and a number of lakes. One of the best known and best-appointed ski resorts in Slovakia is Donovaly, situated on the eastern edge of the Veľká Fatra. The excellent conditions for both downhill and cross-

sort. After the High Tatras and the Western Tatras, it is the third highest mountain range in Slovakia, and, with the former two, the only mountain groups that exceed 2000m. Thanks to the extensive unspoiled forests, the precious karst areas, caves and rock formations as well as the rare species of flora and fauna to be found there, the Low Tatras were declared a national park in 1978. This, the largest national park in Slovakia, is still the

Almost 100-kilometres long, the Low Tatras are Slovakia's longest mountain range.

Adventure in the countryside

Offering Slovakia's best skiing slopes, great hiking trails and climbing and paragliding conditions, the Low Tatras attract lovers of outdoor pursuits all the year round.

home today to bear, wolf, lynx and other animals which disappeared from western Europe some time ago. The most prized part of the Low Tatras is its central part with Chopok (2,024 m) and Ďumbier (2,043 m), the highest peaks of the range. This area is also the best-equipped in terms of infrastructure. The southern and northern slopes of Chopok are home to ski resorts which are considered to be the best in Slovakia. One of Slovakia's most beautiful valleys is the 12km long Demänovská dolina valley, running from the north up to the ski resort

of Jasná at the foot of Chopok. The lower section of the valley is narrow and rich in karstic formations, while the ski resort is located in its upper wider section. Here also is the only mountain lake in the Low Tatras – the Velické pleso – hidden deep in the forest. In the lower section of the valley, the river Demänovka in the past created a network of 30 caves more than 33 km in length, forming one of the world's longest cave systems. Three caves, one of them an ice-cave, are open to the public. The ice-cave was known as early as 1299 and it was surveyed for the first time by Georg Buchholz in 1723. The best known cave, and one of the most stunning stalactite and stalagmite caves in Europe, is Demänovská jaskyňa slobody (Demänovská Cave of Freedom), with spacious caverns on five levels, a rich variety of stalactites and stalagmites of different shapes and colours, and a number of small lakes. The natural beauty, numerous attractions, the ski resort, thermal springs and high quality accommodation make the Demänovská dolina valley one of the best holiday places in Slovakia. Several promising resorts are currently under development on the southern side of the range in and around the Bystrianska dolina valley, where the resort of Tále boasts a new golf course, currently the best in Slovakia, named Grey Bear. The characteristic feature of the eastern part of the Low Tatras is its deep inaccessible forests, which make a paradise for hunters. Although equally beautiful, this part of the mountains has not become a favourite tourist destination due to its less-developed infrastructure. Besides

The highest mountain in the Low Tatras is Ďumbier (2043 m).

The 33-km-long system of caves underneath the mountain is one of the longest in the world.

hikers, the area also attracts canoeing and rafting enthusiasts, as the river Čierny Váh, which, especially in spring, becomes a wild torrent, has its source here. The highest peak of this part of the Low Tatras, offering magnificent panoramic views of the High Tatras, is Kráľova hoľa (1,948), the subject of many legends. Both in winter and in summer, the Low Tatras offer unlimited possibilities to sports enthusiasts.

Marked trails

Paths marked by different colours depending on their difficulty have a long tradition in Slovakia. Signposts indicate the time needed to get to the nearest destinations, altitudes and information about bus and railway connections.

Orava Castle

On a 120-metre-high rock over the river Orava in the north of Slovakia stands the monumental and brooding, but yet majestic Gothic-Renaissance Orava Castle. Its strategic location on the main road between the Hungarian Kingdom and Poland made it one of the most important castles in the northern Slovak region of Orava. The castle was built in the mid-13th century on the site of an older and smaller wooden castle. The complex was built from the top down. After a lot of construction and reconstruction, three terraces were

Orava Castle is built on a 120-metre-high rock above the meandering Orava River.

The castle consists of a number of different sections with the oldest parts on the top of the rock. In good weather conditions, the castle offers stunning views of the Western Tatras.

The Western Tatras

The Western Tatras lie in the north of Slovakia, bordering the High Tatras in the east. Although the Western Tatras became a part of the Tatra National Park in 1987, they are not a homogeneous part of the High Tatras and their development has been different. They form a vast natural barrier between Poland and Slovakia with approximately a quarter of the mountain range being on Polish territory. On the Slovak side, the Western Tatras can be accessed from the historical regions of Liptov and Orava. In comparison with the High Tatras, the Western Tatras are much

created, representing three stand-alone castles interlinked to form a single monumental fortress, which gained its present form in the 17th century. The fortress-like look of the castle is reinforced by massive fortifications with a tunnel and casemates. In 1800 the castle burnt down, but conservation works began soon after to prevent its decay. The castle's last owners – the Pálffy family – contributed to its reconstruction. Thanks to its mysterious appearance, the castle premises were chosen as the setting for the German movie „Nosferatu" in the early days of the film era. The individual castle terraces offer unique views of the Western Tatras and the Orava valley.

Comparable with the High Tatras in terms of their beauty, the Western Tatras are Slovakia's second highest mountain range.

Traditions

The Orava region is famous for its surviving folk traditions and art. The typical local products, especially musical instruments, dishes and toys, are made from wood and other natural materials.

less developed and less well-known as a destination for tourists. With a maximum height of 2,250 m, the Western Tatras are the second highest mountain range in Slovakia, and they compare with the High Tatras in the beauty of their nature. Villages and small tourist centres on the southern, 'Liptov' side of the Western Tatras serve as starting points for tours in the mountains. The valleys leading to the main ridge are covered with deep forests and at the higher altitudes there are some mountain lakes and waterfalls. The woods are home to bear, wolf and lynx, with chamois and marmot living higher in the mountains. The main mountain ridge is ideal for hiking and ski tours, as

Comparable with the High Tatras in terms of their beauty, the Western Tatras are Slovakia's second highest mountain range.

tant tourist centres in the region, attracting water sports enthusiasts. A large aquatic centre, taking its water from thermal springs and open all the year round, has been constructed on its northern edge. From there, it is possible to get to the other side of the Western Tatras, part of the Orava region, by crossing a mountain pass which offers a breathtaking view of the whole Liptov valley. One of the gateways to this part of the mountain range is the village of Zuberec at the entrance to Roháčska dolina – the largest and most beautiful valley of the Western Tatras. The valley, of glacial origin and around 10 km in length, is surrounded by dolomite peaks and provides wonderful conditions for hiking tours and cross-country skiing. It is protected for its rare flora and fauna and there are four mountain lakes and several waterfalls at the end of the valley. Also there is an important ski resort, open until late April thanks to its north-facing slopes. One of the most picturesque museums in Slovakia is the Museum of the Orava Village, built at the entrance to the valley. Its collection holds more than 60 remarkable examples of folk architecture from all over the region. Each August, the local amphitheatre becomes the venue for a folk festival. After a strenuous hike or a day's skiing, a bath in the hot springs of Oravice will certainly do you good, before you set off for a trip to the other beautiful valleys of the Western Tatras.

the differences in altitude are smaller and it is not as steep as the main ridge of the High Tatras. The river Belá, flowing from the southern side of the mountain range and fed by streams in the valleys of the Western Tatras is probably the best river for rafting in Slovakia. Especially in the spring months, when the snow melts off the hills, it turns into a wild torrent full of large boulders. The Belá flows

Hiking and skiing trips

Less jagged than the High Tatras, the valleys and the main ridge of the West Tatras are ideal for hiking and ski touring. Thanks to its northern orientation and cold winters, the mountains' only ski resort offers great conditions for skiers long into the spring.

close to the village of Pribylina, where the Museum of the Liptov Village is located, featuring precious buildings from the villages that were flooded during the construction of one of Slovakia's largest reservoirs– Liptovská Mara. At the Museum, you can visit and admire typical wooden houses from the past centuries, rare churches and a medieval manor house. Many activities bringing in holidaymakers from the area are organised there during the year. The Liptovská Mara reservoir is one of the most impor-

Traditional architecture

Situated at the foot of the Western Tatras, the outdoor Museum of the Orava Village displays traditional houses and buildings from all over the region. Every August, the amphitheatre hosts a folklore festival.

EASTERN SLOVAKIA

Medieval towns
Majestic peaks
Underground world
Wooden churches

High Tatras

The High Tatras are a unique alpine mountain range in the north of the country on the border with Poland. Although covering a relatively small area, the High Tatras are the highest part of the entire Carpathian chain and of this region of Europe. Due to the absence of any foothills, the High Tatras resemble a high granite wall rising from the broad basin of Popradská kotlina, with a difference in altitude of 2,000 m. The whole mountain group is of roughly the same height with 25 peaks exceeding 2,500 m. The highest peak of Slovakia, and of the whole Carpathian range, is Gerlachovský štít (2,655). The High Tatras form Slovakia's most important all-year-round tourist attraction. For many people they are the symbol of Slovakia, and the Slovaks are rightly proud of them. The High Tatras are the only genuinely alpine mountains in Slovakia and are markedly different from all the other mountain ranges. In their relatively small area are concentrated a number of natural beauties of all kinds and, thanks to its relief, visitors can readily get to breathtaking scenery of glaciated valleys with rare flora and fauna in a very short period of time. The mountains' 35 valleys hold more than 100 peri-glacial lakes as a reminder of past gla-

The High Tatras are the only truly alpine mountain range in Slovakia.

Resorts in the High Tatras fit well into the beautiful scenery. Their boom period was in the 19th century.

The High Tatras are noted for their mountain huts.

real development began only after the opening of the railway in the High Tatras in 1871. It was in the following period that new settlements were founded, creating the chain of villages below the mountains that we know today. At first, visitors used to come for medical treatment and most of the early buildings were sanatoria. By the end of the century, the best known centres were Štrbské Pleso in the west, Starý Smokovec in the centre and Tatranská Lomnica in the eastern part of the High Tatras. Further development was brought about by connecting the settlements to the railway. Starting in 1895, all the important settlements were inter-connected by 1912. The greater accessibility brought more people who, besides the health treatment, wanted also to see the mountains, and tourists started to arrive. Hotels, lodging houses and private villas were built including the largest and most luxurious Grand Hotels, built by the Belgian company Wagons

ciers. The deep forests and valleys are home to many protected species, including at the lower altitudes, bear, wolf, lynx and otter. Chamois and marmot can be seen higher in the mountains and eagles nest high above them on inaccessible rocky peaks. In order to better preserve this natural treasure, in 1949 the High Tatras were declared the first national park in Slovakia.

The first reference to exploring the High Tatras dates from 1565 when the Duchess Beata Laski of Kežmarok Castle set out for a trip to the mountains. The first description of a climb to one of Tatra peaks comes from David Fröhlich, a scientist from Kežmarok, who did so in 1615.

The porters

Carrying provisions to the inaccessible mountain huts has a long tradition in the Tatras. In a single ascent often taking up to several hours, a porter is able to carry as much as 100 kg of provisions up the steep slope to the hut. Thanks to these enthusiasts, draft beer is on sale even at the higher altitudes.

Many others followed their example before the first foreign adventurers came to discover the High Tatras. Although the oldest settlement in the High Tatras - Starý Smokovec, originally Schmecks, was founded back in 1793 as a spa, it wasn't until the 19th century that tourists began to flock here in any numbers . However, the

The High Tatras rear up without foothills more than 2000 m above the surrounding countryside.

Lits Cook between 1904 and 1906. From the moment of their construction, the hotels have been the dominant features of the High Tatras tourist centres. The health resorts gradually turned into winter sports centres. Many sports facilities were built, including a toboggan run, skating rinks, tennis courts, golf course and a horseracing track. By the end of the 19th century, the first hiking trails leading high up into the mountains were marked. The total length of these trails today is almost 360 km. The prospect of more and more tourists getting up into the alpine environment made the construction of mountain huts and shel-

The village of Ždiar with typical painted wooden houses.

Rich flora

Unlike the granite High Tatras, the Belianske Tatras are formed from limestone. The nutrient-rich soil nourishes a multitude of plant species.

ters a necessity. The highest located hut, at 2,015m open throughout the year, is the Téryho chata, built in 1899. Back in 1935, Štrbské pleso was the venue for the World Nordic Skiing Championship. In 1940 a cable-car to Lomnický štít, at 2,632m the second highest peak in the High Tatras, came into operation, holding several world records until 1958. Hosting the World Nordic Skiing Champion-

ship again in 1970 led to a further development boom in the High Tatras with the construction of new hotels and infrastructure .

In the east, the High Tatras neighbour on to the Belianske Tatras, which, unlike the granite High Tatras, are a predominantly limestone mountain range. Although the

Proud of traditions

The inhabitants of Ždiar take pride in their traditions and richly decorated costumes. The local dialect has similarities to Polish.

smallest of the Tatra mountain groups, due to their geological composition they have the largest variety of flora. The karst area of Belianske Tatry is rich in caves, of which only Belianska jaskya with its beautiful stalactites is accessible to the public. It was opened to the public in 1882, although inscriptions on the cave walls attest that it was already well-known in the 18th century. In contrast with the other settlements in the vicinity of the mountains, the village of Ždiar, situated under the two highest peaks of the Belianske Tatras (2,152m), was founded by shepherds in the 17th century. Its vivid folklore and well-preserved folk architecture, with typical wooden houses decorated with colourful ornaments, are the typical features of the village.

The characteristic scattered settlements.

The local people, who speak a distinctive dialect, mostly make a living from providing services to tourists attracted to a well-known skiing resort.

Spišská Sobota

Nowadays, Spišská Sobota is a part of Poprad (population 56,000), the commercial and administrative centre of the area near the Tatras. It was formed by merging several previously separate towns in the Spiš region. The first mention of Poprad dates from 1256. It was one of 15 towns of

The most important monument is St. George's Church in the middle of the square.

the Spiš region which between 1412 and 1772 belonged to Poland. The town became more important in the 19th century after the construction of the railway, followed by the development of industry and tourism. Poprad, as we know it today, was formed in the 20th century as a result of a merger of independent towns such as Spišská Sobota, Matejovce, Veká and Stráže. Nowadays, Poprad is the gateway to the High Tatras and benefits from the development of tourism in the region. In addition to the mountains and historical monuments, it has a new aquatic centre fed from a thermal spring, and many attractions open throughout the year.Until the 19th century, Spišská Sobota had a dominant position among the towns which are now parts of Poprad. This well-preserved town, famous for its craftsmen, stayed untouched by the influenc-

es of the 20th century and now, after reconstruction, is a favourite destination for lovers of history and art. Spišská Sobota was granted a municipal charter in 1271 and until the 20th century, in common with other towns of the Spiš region, its inhabitants were the 'Spiš' Germans Twice the town was destroyed by fire, in 1545 and 1775. Following

The interior of the church conceals a real treasure – five precious Gothic altars.

In the square of Spišská Sobota there are a number of houses that once belonged to local craftsmen.

its reconstruction after the last fire, its architecture has not changed. Its most noted monument is the Church of St George, standing at the highest point of the extended square, with burgher houses from the 16th and 17th centuries with the shingle saddle roofs typical of the Spiš region, on the sides of the square. Built in the 13th century, the church was reconstructed in the 15th century in the Gothic style. Its interior is well preserved, including real treasures in the form of five valuable late Gothic altars from the 15th and 16th centuries. The main altar (1516) was carved by Master Pavol of Levoča. In the vicinity of the church there is a Renaissance bell tower dating from 1598, later rebuilt in the baroque style typical of the Spiš region. The town of Spišská Sobota has recently experienced a revival as a tourist destination, thanks to the fact that the former burgher houses have been converted into cosy hotels and lodging houses.

Kežmarok 🏨

Kežmarok (population 18,000), one of historical centres of the Spiš region, lies in the foothills of

The biggest building in Kežmarok is the fourteenth-century Gothic castle.

the High Tatras. It was formed by the merger of three settlements in the 13th century and was granted a municipal charter as early as 1269. The town's boom period came when the German settlers took advantage of its position on a trade route from the east to the north of Europe and began to develop trade and craft there. By the 15th century, Kežmarok had more than 40 guilds, which made it one of the best developed towns

Bell Towers in Spiš

Renaissance bell towers erected next to churches are typical of most of the towns in the Spiš region. Many of them are still decorated with sgrafitto.

in then Hungarian Kingdom. Between 1358 and 1570, the town was involved in the so-called '200-year-war' with the neighbouring town of Levoča for the right of storage – one of the sources of wealth of medieval towns. The Town Castle, situated near the centre of Kežmarok, was originally built as a Gothic castle in the 14th century, with fortifications connecting it with the town. At the turn of the 16th century, when it was owned by the Thököly family, it was refashioned to its present day form in a Renaissance style. The most remarkable part of the castle is its chapel, which was renovated in 1658. Typical Gothic, Renaissance and ba-

Another landmark of Kežmarok is the Gothic Church of the Holy Cross from the 15th century.

roque houses of artisans and merchants have been preserved in the streets of Kežmarok. Among other prominent features of the town is the Gothic Church of the

Holy Cross from the 15th century, with its interior including Gothic altars from the school of Master Pavol of Levoča. One of the most beautiful Renaissance bell towers in Spiš, built in 1591, with well-preserved sgraffito decoration, stands next to the church. It was built at a period when the church belonged to Protestants (1548-1673). One of the monuments of the town is the Town Hall, originally built in the Gothic style and reconstructed in the Renaissance style after a fire in the 16th century. After a subsequent fire in the 18th

The unique wooden Protestant Church holds up to 1500 worshippers.

century, it was rebuilt in the classical style to give it its present day form. The most beautiful burgher houses surround the ridotto from 1808 near the Town Hall. Other sights in Kežmarok include the Protestant houses built outside the town's gate. The attractive Protestant Church was built without a single nail in 1717 by carpenters from northern Europe. Its precious wooden interior, with early baroque paintings and a wooden organ, can hold more than 1500 people. The nearby Protestant seminary from the 18th century, founded as early as 1531, houses a school library with 150,000 volumes, established in 1776. The adjoining Protestant Church, built in an unusual oriental style on the basis of the project by Theophil von Hansen,

Protestant Church

Built in 1717, this church is one of Kežmarok's landmarks. As the laws at the time only allowed Protestants to build their places of worship from wood and outside the town's boundaries, the church, including the organ, was built entirely from wood without a single nail.

the architect of the Parliament building in Vienna, features the burial chapel of Imrich Thököly, the leader of one of the anti-Habsburg uprisings.

Kežmarok is associated with the first explorations of the High Tatras. Beata Laski, the duchess of Kežmarok Castle, organised the first recorded trip to the mountains in 1565. Even today, Kežmarok is one of the starting points for trips to the High Tatras. The town's rich artisan tradition is commemorated at the beginning of July each year by the largest craft fair in Slovakia, an attraction for the developing tourism of the region.

Strážky

One sight in the Kežmarok area which is worth a visit is the manor house of Strážky. This small town was founded as a strong-point on the trade route to Poland and is among the oldest in the area. In 1556

The sixteenth-century Renaissance manor of Strážky is not far from Kežmarok.

the king gave it to Marcus Horvath Stansith de Gradecz as a reward for his achievements in the wars against the Turks. The manor house was built in the Renaissance style between the years 1570 and 1590 by his son Gregor Horvath, by combining two bastions of the older Gothic castle from the 15th century. The widely educated Gregor Horvath founded what was, for those times, a progressive Protestant upper school, which functioned from 1584 until 1711 and served to prepare children from aristocratic families for their university studies. The fourth wing and arcades were added in the 18th century. Ladislav Mednyánszky (1852-1919), a descendant who lived part of his life at the manor, later became a landscape and portrait painter well known throughout Europe. The manor now features paintings of Ladislav Mednyánszky and the valuable library

Levoča is noted for its mix of different types of architecture.

of Baron Eduard Mednyánszky, and belongs to the Slovak National Gallery. A large English park surrounds the manor house.

Levoča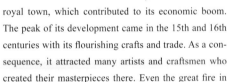

Levoča (population 10,000), one of the best-preserved historical towns in Slovakia, is situated to the east of the High Tatras, in the heart of the Spiš region. A relatively small territory, the Spiš region is noted throughout Slovakia for its high concentration of artistic, historical and architectural monuments, and its pearl, the town of Levoča, has yet to be discovered by foreign visitors.

The town owed much of its wealth to its favoured location on the important trade route to Poland and to the German settlers, invited here by the king, who were able to take advantage of the location. In the 13th century, Levoča came to be the most important town in the Spiš region and in 1271 it became the seat of the union of 24 Spiš towns. In the beginning of the 14th century, it became a free royal town, which contributed to its economic boom. The peak of its development came in the 15th and 16th centuries with its flourishing crafts and trade. As a consequence, it attracted many artists and craftsmen who created their masterpieces there. Even the great fire in 1550, which destroyed many Gothic buildings and the town's precious archives, could not put an end to the boom, and the reconstruction that ensued adopted the new, Renaissance style. With its book printing and publishing, the town became a centre of the Reformation. The anti-Habsburg movement in the 17th and 18th centuries ushered in a period of decline, which was increased by the omission of Levoča from the route of the main railway in 1871. Nevertheless, as a result of this stagnation, the town has

In the middle of the square are the Renaissance Old Town Hall and the Gothic St. James' Church.

Levoča is one of Slovakia's best-preserved medieval towns.

Church of St James was built at the end of the 14th century and is now the second largest Gothic church in Slovakia. The entire interior of the building is unique and well preserved. The state of preservation of the 14th century wall paintings, the first cycle of 14 images depicting the seven cardinal virtues and the seven deadly sins — and the second cycle illustrating the Legend of Dorothy in 20 scenes is really astounding. However, these works of art of great value are put in the shade by the 15 mostly Gothic and Renaissance altars of immense artistic, historical, material and aesthetic importance. Five of them are works of Master Pavol of Levoča who, along with the likes of Riemenschneider, Stoss and Pacher, is one of the greatest woodcarvers of the late Gothic period in central Europe. His masterpiece is the 18.6m high and 6m wide main altar, carved from wood between 1507 and 1517,

retained its original appearance and its unique artistic and architectural monuments. Well-preserved medieval fortifications surround the town, enclosing the dominant central square featuring St. James' Church, the Old Town Hall and the Protestant Church. The Parish

St. James' Church houses a number of valuable artefacts. The main altar is the world's highest Gothic altar.

Master Pavol

A prominent central-European wood-carver of the late-Gothic period, Master Pavol of Levoča is the author of many precious altars in the churches in central and eastern Slovakia.

the tallest preserved Gothic altar in the world.

Alongside the church there is a marvellous Gothic and Renaissance Old Town Hall completed between 1551 and 1559. The building's most beautiful room is its large council hall, designed in the Renaissance style. The nearby belfry dating from the 17th century became a part of the Old Town Hall in the 18th century. On the perimeter of the building is the 16th century so-called 'cage of shame' in which accused criminals were locked and exposed to public. Another notable monument in the centre of the square is the large Protestant church, built in the classical style between 1825 and 1837. On the sides of the square stand more than 60 houses of wealthy tradesmen, built in the 14th and 15th century. The most outstanding is the Thurzo House, built by joining two Gothic houses in the 16th century. The rich sgraffito decoration on the facade of the house dates back to the beginning of the 20th century. At the rear of the church stands the House of Master Pavol, originally a Gothic house from the 15th century, later with a Renaissance façade added, today a museum. The notable Krupek House with remarkable façade paintings dating from the 16th century is opposite the Old Town Hall. At least three of the houses on the square – the Mariássy's, Spillenberger's and Schwab's, now a hotel – have retained their pleasant Renaissance arcaded courtyards. A large section of the town's fortifications, dating from the period between the 14th and 17th centuries, in a total length of 2 km with 6 bastions and 3 gates, has been preserved and forms the town silhouette. A way-marked trail leads to Mariánsky kopec (Mary's Hill) above the town, with the Basilica Minor. Originally a chapel for pilgrims, today it is the object of the most important pilgrimage for Slovakia's worshippers. During the communist regime, this pilgrimage represented the largest anti-communist mass-protest. Pope John Paul II took part in the pilgrimage here in 1995.

Spiš Castle

Covering an area of four hectares, Spiš Castle forms one of the biggest complexes of its kind in central Europe. The oldest part of the compound is the tall circular tower and the Romanesque palace, built in the beginning of the 13th century. Together with the chapel, added

St. Martin's Cathedral in Spišská Kapitula.

Spiš Castle, one of the biggest castle complexes in central Europe, can be seen from a long distance.

in the 15th century during a massive reconstruction of the Romanesque building, these make up the so-called Upper Castle, which is the only section of the complex where the original rooms have been preserved. The castle was the property of the king until 1464 when it was given to the Zápolya family. After the Battle of Mohacs in 1526, the Zápolyas were one of the fiercest rivals of the emerging Habsburgs. The castle is the birthplace of

An interesting silhouette of the Church of the Holy Spirit in Žehra.

John Zápolya, the last king of Hungary prior to the accession of the Habsburgs. At the beginning of the 18th century, the last owners of the castle – the Csáky family – moved to nearby manors in Hodkovce and Bijacovce and the castle became neglected. The final blow came in 1780 when the complex was engulfed in a great fire. The military garrison stationed here left and the once mighty Spiš Castle was abandoned and fell into ruins. On the hill opposite the castle is the monastic compound of Spišská Kapitula. The origins of this place go back to the 11th century when it was the site of a fortified Benedictine monastery. From the end of the 12th century it served as the seat of the Provost of Spiš and it has been the centre of the bishopric since 1776. Visitors to this unique church town can admire the preserved canons' houses, the Episcopal Palace, seminary, cathedral, as well as the mid-17th century ramparts. To this day, Spišská Kapitula has retained its sacred character; the visitor has the impression that time stopped here a long time ago. The town and its surroundings are dominated by one of the most important places of worship in Slovakia, the Romanesque-Gothic St. Martin's Cathedral, 1245- 1275.

Over the centuries, new chapels were added to the main building and it was subject to especially heavy reconstruction in the 15th century. In 1488-99, the Zápolya family erected a funeral chapel in the Gothic style. The interior of the cathedral boasts five unique altars from the second half of the 15th century and precious frescoes from 1317 depicting the coronation of the King of Hungary, Robert of Anjou. Another unique artefact is the thirteenth-century stone sculpture of a white lion, the so-called 'Leo Albus', one of the oldest carvings of its kind in Slovakia. The sculpture was originally placed in the southern portal of the cathedral, now non-existent. The Episcopal Palace, situated opposite the cathedral, was originally a thirteenth-century Romanesque building. Over the centuries it was subject to various reconstructions and acquired its present shape between 1753 and 1766. In this unique church town's only street, there

Majestic medieval paintings cover most of the building's interior.

are a number of attractive houses with interesting details on their facades, and the Bell Tower dating from 1739, through which it was possible to enter the French gardens of the Episcopal Palace. Close to Spiš Castle is an attractive hiking location – the travertine hill Dreveník, protected as a UNESCO Biosphere Reserve. Tourists following the marked trail between the steep 50-metre-high cliffs can admire the unique flora, as well as the gorgeous vistas over the castle. In good weather conditions, even the jagged peaks of the High Tatras are visible. Within sight of Spiš Castle, behind the Dreveník hill, is the village of Žehra, renowned for its Church of the Holy Spirit from 1245-1275, bearing typical traces of the transitional period between the Romanesque and Gothic styles. The characteristic onion-shaped tower dates back to the 18th century. The church is especially significant for the gems in its interior. Much of the church's interior – the whole chancel and large parts of the nave –is covered with magnificent Byzantine-style iconographic frescoes made by Italian masters between the 13th and 15th centuries. In 1993, the Romanesque-Gothic buildings at Spiš Castle and in the neighbouring Spišská Kapitula and Žehra were added to the UNESCO World Heritage List.

Spišská Nová Ves

Slovakia's tallest church tower (87m).

Nowadays one of the biggest towns in the Spiš region, in the Middle Ages Spišská Nová Ves (population 40,000) was overshadowed by the more dynamic towns of Levoča and Kežmarok. The town was co-founded by German colonists invited by king Béla IV to help reconstruct the country's economy following the Tartar invasions. The oldest written reference to Spišská Nová Ves (at that time called Villa Nova) dates back to 1268. At that time the town belonged to the union of 24 towns of the Spiš region. Enjoying privileges granted by the king, the economic development of Spišská Nová Ves continued apace with mining as the dominant economic activity. Between 1412 and 1772, Spišská Nová Ves and 15 other towns in this region were held by Poland as security for a loan granted to the Hungarian king. Upon the return of the province to Hungary, Spišská Nová Ves became its capital. The town received an impetus for further growth with its connection to the main railway in 1871. The elongated square in the centre of the town is one of the longest in Slovakia. Built on a west-east axis, one side of the square always gets the sun and the other the shade, hence the sides are called the "Summer Street" and the "Winter Street". In the middle of the square is the town's landmark – the Gothic-style parish church. From its 87-metre-high tower, the highest church tower in Slovakia, in good weather conditions one can see the High Tatras. The building was reconstructed a couple of times in the 15th century after suffering damage in a fire and an earthquake. Despite these catastrophes, unique Gothic artefacts, including those by Master Pavol of Levoča, have survived in the interior of the church. Other treasures include the Renaissance frescoes from the early 16th century and the exquisite Gothic southern portal. Not far from the church, in the middle of the square, is the Protestant Church built in the classical style on the site of an older wooden church

The Provincial House with richly decorated rococo façade.

St. Ladislas' Church in Spišský Štvrtok.

windows, on the ornamented façade of the house, there are six famous allegorical reliefs depicting rules of conduct for civil servants.

To get a taste of the town's traditional atmosphere, the best time for a visit is July, when the historical Spiš market takes place. Spišská Nová Ves is also a great starting point for hikes to one of the most beautiful parts of the country – the Slovenský raj (Slovak Paradise) National Park. Only a few kilometres to the west is the village of Spišský Štvrtok with a prominent church spire standing above the surrounding countryside. The Church of St Ladislas already stood on this site before the Tartar invasions in the years 1241-42 and was rebuilt in the 15th century. Its architecture is characteristic of the transitional period between the Romanesque and Gothic styles. In 1473, a two-storey funeral chapel of the Zápolya family was added. Inspired by la Sainte Chapelle in Paris, the builder of the church – the renowned architect Hans Puchsbaum – created one of the finest Gothic buildings in Slovakia.

at the end of the 18th century. Another elegant classical building is the 18th century Town Hall with a two-storey ceremonial hall. One of the town's most beautiful buildings is the Art-Nouveau Reduta, built at the turn of the 20th century. This domed building with two towers is currently the seat of the Spiš Theatre. The most prominent of the richly decorated houses in the square is the Provincial House. Once a Town Hall, this house was built in the Middle Ages, and reconstructed in the rococo style in the years 1763-65 to serve as the seat of the regional authority of the province of the 16 Spiš towns. Between the

Spišský Štvrtok

St. Ladislav's Church is one of the most significant architectural monuments of Spiš. From the top of the church hill one can see far into the distance. The architecture of the church is characteristic of the transitional period between the Romanesque and the Gothic styles.

The façade of the Markušovce Manor.

Markušovce

A few kilometres east of Spišská Nová Ves is the historical village of Markušovce with a beautiful manor house once belonging to the Mariássy family. The palace with four circular turrets at its corners was built in the Renaissance style in 1643. Its façade was given rich rococo decoration in 1770-75 and a turret was added

The Dardanela garden pavilion was built in expectation of the visit of Emperor Joseph II.

in the same style. When it was announced in 1778 that the heir to the throne, Joseph II, was planning a visit to Markušovce, work began on the construction of the rococo-style Dardanely pavilion at the end of the terraced French garden behind the palace. Joseph II never made it to Markušovce and consequently only the middle part of the pavilion was finished. The side parts of the building, now used for concerts, were finished in the 1970s. In addition to the well-preserved rococo wall paintings in the Dardanela pavilion, visitors can also admire the exhibition of historical furniture in the manor, featuring some exhibits from Spiš Castle.

Wild nature

The moist climate makes the national park an ideal habitat for plants, which attract different types of insects. A paradise for butterflies and butterfly-lovers – there are more than 2,100 butterfly species in Slovenský raj.

Slovenský raj 🌲 🏵️

To the east of the majestic Low Tatra mountain range lies one of the smallest protected natural areas in Slovakia, the Slovenský raj (Slovak Paradise) National Park. The region may lack high summits, but, as its name indicates, it is one of the most beautiful parts of the country. It has deep ravines and canyons cut into the limestone terrain by numerous streams, and is covered in dense forest, which provides a habitat for large predators, including brown bear, wolf, lynx and wild cat.

Hikers heading into Slovenský raj usually start in one of three villages on the outskirts of the park, all of which offer a good choice of accommodation.

Way-marked trails starting in the villages of Podlesok and Čingov lead through gorges and canyons to the central

The trails in narrow ravines often follow the riverbeds directly.

plateau. The trails follow the mountain streams that flow from the plateau through gorges which can be up to 200 m deep and often only a metre wide. It is not an easy terrain for walking, as the trails often follow the stream-bed directly and a number of ladders need to be climbed in order to negotiate waterfalls which can be anything up to 100 m high. Because the terrain is so difficult, many of the ravines are only negotiable in one direction - upstream. Thanks to the plentiful water supply and the high humidity, there is lush vegetation with plenty of rare plants that attract more than 2,100 butterfly species - the highest number of butterflies found anywhere in Slovakia.

Besides the log rafts, one can also explore the beautiful Pieniny region on foot or bicycle.

with a temperature of 24°C, were popular with the Polish and Hungarian nobility. At the end of the 19th century, the spa, along with Stará Ľubovňa Castle, was bought by Count Zamojski from Poland who modernised it with the help of his wife, Princess Caroline de Bourbon. The work commenced by the Count was completed by his son, with the financial support of his wife, Isabella de Bourbon. The richest spring in the spa now bears the lady's name. The resort's most interesting swimming pool is the 20-metre wide lake formed in a crater.

when their order was dissolved during the Reformation. In 1705, the monastery was given to the Camaldolese order from Italy, who focused mainly on education and science. Červený kláštor was made famous by the monk Cyprian, a dedicated botanist and healer, who founded one of the first pharmacies in this part of the country.

Cyprian collected medicinal plants and created a unique herbarium, which is now on display in the museum. Written in four languages, the herbarium lists 272 plants with descriptions of their healing properties and procedures for their use in treating various maladies. Cyprian was also known as the 'flying monk', as he endeavoured to construct a flying machine. Unfortunately, no records of his engineering activities have been preserved, because many documents were destroyed in a fire in 1782. Abandoned in ruins for more than a century, this unique monastic compound was reconstructed after WW2. Within the protective walls can be seen the Gothic Church of St. Anthony, the fourteenth-century monastery and reconstructed houses of the monks, as well as the pharmacy. The traditional folklore festival, held in the village of Červený Kláštor every June, is a great opportunity for observing the rich folk traditions of this unique region in northern Spiš. After a strenuous trek in the mountains, weary hikers can give their bodies a rest in the nearby Vyšné Ružbachy spa, founded in the 15th century. In the past, these springs,

Bardejov

Slovakia's best-preserved medieval town Bardejov (population 33,000) was established on a trade route to Poland in the 13th century. In 1376 it became a free town by royal charter and the ensuing two centuries came to be viewed as the town's golden age, as far as fame and wealth are concerned. The town owed its development mainly to German tradesmen and to its flourishing trades – in its heyday, the town could number more than 50 guilds. Many historical buildings from this era have been preserved up to the present, furnishing Bardejov with

The Old Town Hall and St. Egidius' Church in Bardejov.

In 2000, Slovakia's best-preserved medieval town was added to the list of UNESCO World Heritage Sites.

its unique medieval atmosphere. Bardejov is surrounded by ramparts, with 11 bastions and two gates built in the 14th-16th century, preserved almost intact. The picturesque central square, flanked by Gothic and Renaissance burgher houses, is dominated by the Gothic St. Egidius' Cathedral from the 15th century. The interior of the grand cathedral contains priceless artefacts, including 11 Gothic altars from 1460 – 1520 still standing in their original po-

Architecture of Bardejov

The large central square is flanked by original Gothic houses, mostly with modernised façades. One of the most interesting buildings is the Gantzughof with rococo frescoes.

From inside, the church looks just as it did 500 years ago.

sitions. In the middle of the square is the remarkable Old Town Hall, built in the Gothic-Renaissance style in 1505 -1511. It is the first Renaissance building to be built within the territory of the present-day Slovak Republic. The ground floor of the Old Town Hall used to be the town's market hall and the first floor housed the officials of the municipality. The building is also of interest for the statuette of a man displaying his hindquarters, positioned in the upper part of the building's oriel. Legend has it that it was put there by the architect as a revenge for him not receiving his agreed fee. Among Bardejov's other sights are: the Gantzughof House opposite the Old Town Hall, originally built in the Gothic style and now with rococo frescoes on its façade; the Executioner's House; the Humanist School from the 16th century; the Protestant Church; the 15th-century Franciscan Church; the Greek Catholic Church and the so-called Jewish area with its 19th-century synagogue with a remarkable roof consisting of nine arches. The latest addition to the mosaic of various ethnic groups and religions in the town is the newly- built Orthodox Church. These ethnic groups and religions have, over the centuries, brought cultural diversity to this beautiful part of the country. Bardejov's unique character and excellent state of preservation were acknowledged by UNESCO who added it to its list of World Heritage Sites in 2000. Four kilometres from Bardejov is one of Slovakia's best-known healing resorts – Bardejovské Kúpele. Visited since the 16th century, the spa became especially popular in the 19th century when word of the healing effects

Wooden church from the 18th century in the Lukov village.

The outdoor Museum of Folk Architecture in the Bardejovské Kúpele spa.

of the 17 local springs spread all over Europe. The list of the resort's most prominent guests includes names like the Emperor Joseph II, the second wife of Napoleon I, Marie Louise, the Russian Tsar Alexander I, and the Empress Elisabeth (Sissi), wife of the Emperor Franz Joseph I. The outdoor Museum of Folk Architecture, now popular with the spa guests, features over 30 houses and other examples of local architecture, including the wooden churches for which the region is famous that have been moved here from the surrounding villages.

Wooden Churches

In the north-eastern reaches of Slovakia, near the border with Poland and not far from the towns of Bardejov and Svidník, there are a number of unique wooden churches. The small hamlets scattered over the countryside here are home to Slovakia's Ruthenian minority, an ethnic group which belongs to the Orthodox Uniate church. There are up to 30 protected sacred buildings

in this area, all built between the 15th and 20th centuries. Most of these all-wooden structures were built in the 17th and 18th centuries and belong to the Greek Catholic Church. Architecturally, there are two types of these unique structures: those churches with a single roof and those with three onion-shaped descending towers. A number of these buildings contain precious iconostases and frescoes, which add to the overall aesthetic impression left upon visitors once they enter their twilit interiors. While the most renowned churches are in the villages of Lukov, Kožany, Bodružal, Ladomirová and Miroľa, the

Many local churches have three onion-shaped towers.

Decorative iconostases inside the churches.

One of Prešov's landmarks – the Gothic Church of St. Nicholas.

oldest one of all is the Gothic Roman Catholic Church of St George in Hervartov, dating from around 1500. Typically, these exceptional sacred buildings are located on a hill a little away from the village and surrounded by tall old trees. They are the products of the artistry and vision of past unknown craftsmen of great skill and imagination. This is also the area where the parents of the famous American pop-artist Andy Warhol came from.

Prešov 🏰

Prešov (population 93,000), Slovakia's third biggest city and an important cultural and business centre of the north-eastern part of Slovakia, lies only about 30

The Greek Catholic Cathedral and the Episcopal Palace in Prešov.

kilometres north of its big eastern-Slovak neighbour, Košice. The history of the first settlements in the territory follows a similar pattern to elsewhere in Slovakia. The Slavs settled here sometime between the 8th and 9th centuries and later mixed with colonisers of Hungarian (11th-12th centuries) and German (13th century) origin. In 1299, Prešov was granted municipal rights and in 1374 it was accorded the status of a free royal town. At that time, the town's prosperity was based mainly on its crafts and the trade with Poland. The town suffered many hardships during the anti-Habsburg uprisings in the 17th and 18th centuries, as it changed sides several times. After crushing the uprising led by Imrich Thököly in 1687, the Imperial General Caraffa had 24 protestant burghers executed in the incident known as the „Prešov Slaughter,„. The historical centre of Prešov has retained its character from the town's golden era in the

15th-17th centuries. Like most other towns in eastern Slovakia, the centre is a wide rectangular main street flanked by attractive burgher houses The dominant feature of the square is the fourteenth-century Gothic Ca-

Much of Prešov's main street is a pedestrian zone.

thedral of St. Nicholas, whose interior boasts one of the most beautiful Baroque altars in Slovakia, as well as a number of Gothic artefacts made by Master Pavol of Levoča. The adjoining buildings on the north side are the Protestant College, once an important educational institution, and the Protestant Church, both built in the 17th century. On the south side is the pretty Neptune Fountain

Synagogue

The nineteenth-century Orthodox Synagogue in Prešov is one of the best-preserved buildings of its kind in Slovakia. Today it houses a Museum of Jewish Culture.

from 1738. Other architecturally valuable buildings in the Main Street include the 16th-century Rákóczi Palace, with its upper storey in the typical eastern-Slovak Renaissance style, and the Town Hall, originally built in the Renaissance style, on the opposite side of the street. Other significant monuments serve to illustrate the town's religious diversity: for example, the complex of beautiful buildings including the Greek Catholic Cathedral of St. John the Baptist, the Episcopal Palace, and the 18th-century Greek Catholic Theological Faculty, all in the south-

Caraffa's Prison

Built in 1501 as an armoury, the building was the place where in 1687 the Imperial General Antonio Caraffa tortured the ringleaders of a revolt against the Habsburgs.

ern part of the historical centre. Visitors to Prešov should also not leave out the Orthodox Church of St Alexander Nevský from the beginning of the 20th century, the recently renovated Orthodox Synagogue with a Museum of Jewish Culture in the northern part of the city centre, and the section of the town's fortifications with bastions remaining from the 14th-15th centuries.

Košice

The metropolis of eastern Slovakia and counterpart and counterpoint to the nation's capital Bratislava, Košice (240,000) is the second largest city in Slovakia and an important cultural, scientific and commercial centre. The favourable natural conditions here attracted the first settlers in the Stone Age. The place was occupied in the 8th and the 9th centuries by a Slavic tribe who lived here in a fortified settlement. The first monasteries, at that time functioning as cultural centres, were established here in the 11th-13th centuries and Košice's growth was given a boost by the arrival of German settlers in the 13th century. At around the same time, Košice was granted munic-

14th century Franciscan Church on the main street.

The park behind the building of the State Theatre is one of Košice's cosiest places.

towns. Resembling more a broad boulevard than a square, the one-kilometre-long Main Square is surrounded by interesting sights. The town's centrepoint is the high Gothic St. Elisabeth's Cathedral, named after the daughter of the King of Hungary Andrew II, who was famous for her acts of mercy, and was later canonised.

The construction of the cathedral, the biggest Gothic church in Slovakia and one of the biggest sacred buildings in central Europe, was begun in 1378 and completed in three stages. It was modelled on the Church of St. Victor in the German town of Xanten, as a basilica with five naves. The last part of the building to be finished was the presbytery, completed in 1508. The cathedral was partial-

ipal rights (1290) and in 1342 it became a free royal town. The town's golden age in the 15th century, when Košice was a centre for trade and crafts and one of the biggest towns in the whole of Hungary, was followed by a period of stagnation caused by the Turkish invasion. The town recovered in the 17th century, a period marked by the establishment of a university (1675) that later became the Royal Academy. The connection of Košice to the railway

Urban's Bell Tower

One of the smaller buildings in the middle of Košice's long main square is Urban's Bell Tower, built in the Gothic style. The arcades on the ground floor were added later.

and the development of industry in the 19th century heralded the town's revival. Košice is now home to a number of universities and colleges, scientific institutions, theatres, a philharmonic orchestra, a number of foreign and international companies, all of them giving this city a lively and, given the multi-ethnic origin of its inhabitants, cosmopolitan flavour. The city's central square with a church in the middle is typical of most eastern-Slovak

The spacious interior of the cathedral with the precious main altar from 1477.

ly renovated at the end of the 19th century and in 1906 a crypt was built under the northern nave to house the remains of the leader of the anti-Habsburg uprising, Francis II. Rákoczi, which were brought back from Turkey. In 1556, the church was almost destroyed by fire, but the

St. Elisabeth's Cathedral is Slovakia's largest Gothic church and the pride of Košice.

precious fifteenth-century altars were saved and they can still be seen in the cathedral. The most valuable is the main, late-Gothic altar of St Elisabeth from 1477, with 48 gilded painted panels. An ascent to the top of the tower will be rewarded with a superb view of the whole city.

Next to the cathedral is the fourteenth-century Gothic St Michael's Chapel, originally used as a funeral chapel, and on its other side is Urban's Bell Tower, built in the Gothic style and reconstructed in 1628 in the Renaissance fashion. The final structure in the middle of the square is the neo-Baroque State Theatre built in 1897-1899. The adjacent "singing fountain", with its water pulsating to the rhythm of recorded music, has become an attraction for visitors to Košice and a place of relaxation for the locals. The square is framed by a number of burgher

One of the most interesting buildings in Košice is the nineteenth-century Jakab Palace.

houses, palaces and churches. One of the most important sacred buildings is the Jesuit church and monastery, built for the Jesuit University in 1671-1684 in the manner of Il Gesú Church in Rome. On the same side of the square is the Franciscan church and monastery from the 14th century, reconstructed in the Baroque style in the 18th century. One of the oldest buildings in the square is the late-Gothic Levoča House from the 15th century. Also to be found in the square are a number of beautiful palaces from the 18th and the 19th century, for example, the building of the former Town Hall, the District House, the Episcopal Residence, the Csáky-Dessewffy Palace (the present seat of the Constitutional Court of the Slovak Republic), or the Rákoczi Palace housing the Slovak Technical Museum. Košice's Main Square also includes some examples of the Art Noveau and historicist styles, e.g. the neo-Gothic Jakab Palace near the city's Municipal Park. A number of interesting sights are to be found in the side streets, e.g. the well-preserved houses of craftsmen in Kováska ulica, the Mikluš Prison, one of Košice's best-preserved structures from the Middle Ages built by combining two adjoining houses in the 16th century, or the remains of the town fortifications, including the so-called Hangman's Bastion, erected in the 13th-17th centuries. Visitors to Košice should not miss the unique gold treasure of 3,000 15th-17th century gold coins from all over Europe, on exhibit in the Eastern Slovak Museum. The treasure, weighing 11 kilograms, was discovered in the Rákoczi Palace in 1935.

Jasov

West of Košice, in the direction of the town of Rožňava, lies the village of Jasov, dominated by an impressive Premonstratensian monastery. Erected in

The Premonstratensian monastery in Jasov.

1750-66 according to the designs of Anton Pilgram on the site of an older monastery, the building is suggestive of the High Baroque-style monasteries in Austria and southern Germany, with a church with two towers in the middle dividing the compound into two separate parts with two courtyards. The exquisite decoration of the monastery's interior is the work of a number of artists of repute commissioned by Pilgram. The precious murals in the church and the library (including 80,000 books with

precious incunabuli) were by Johannes Kracker from Vienna. Within the monastic compound there is also a beautiful French garden in the baroque style. Another of Jasov's attractions is the Jasovská cave. Renowned for its abundance of stalactites, pagoda-shaped stalagmites, waterfalls and other natural formations, the cavern is also significant for being home to 19 species of bat. The cave was already known in the 13th century and an inscription dating from 1452 found inside represents the oldest writing ever found in a Slovak cave. The Jasovská cave was the first cave in Slovakia to be opened to the public, by the abbot of the Jasov monastery in 1846. Together with other caves in the Slovak Karst National Park, Jasovská cave became a UNESCO World Heritage listed Site in 1995.

Slovak Karst 🌲 🎴

The mountainous area in the south-eastern part of Slovakia surrounding the historical town of Rožňava is known as the Slovak Karst National Park. Together with the adjoining Aggtelek National Park in Hungary, it forms the largest karstic area in central Europe. Given its abundance of cultural and natural places of interest, it is also one of the most beautiful parts of Slovakia. In 1977, the Slovak Karst received international recognition when it was declared a UNESCO Biosphere Reserve. The Slovak Karst is a mountain area with a number of karstic formations such as dissected plateaux and canyons cut by river erosion into the soft rock. Caves, gorges, chasms and canyons are plentiful, together with rare species of fauna and flora. The place is a natural habitat for more than 1,000 species of butterfly. Up to 50 caves have been explored here, four of which are open to the public. In 1995 they were added, together with ad-

The monastery is surrounded by French gardens in the baroque style.

The unique stalactites in the Gombasecká Cave.

Sections of the 250-metre deep Zádielska tiesňava gorge are only 10 m wide.

joining caves in Hungary, to the list of UNESCO World Heritage Sites. Most significant of all the caves here is Domica. Accessible from both Slovakia and Hungary, this „cross-border" cave is one of the biggest and most beautiful caverns in Europe. Besides being vast (the underground passages are more than 20 kilometres long) it also has a long history –there is evidence of it being occupied more than 6000 years ago. Inside the cavern, visitors are stunned by the vast array of beautiful natural formations including pagoda-shaped stalagmites and a number of cascading lakes. The tour includes a cruise on the eerie waters of the underground river Styx. The nearby Gombasecká cave is interesting for its curious-

ly shaped formations, the most interesting of which are its „straw stalactites" up to 3 metres long but only 2-3 mm thick looking like huge hairs trailing from the cave roof. A few kilometres down the road towards the village of Silica is the almost 100-metre deep Silická Precipice, a cave which has suffered a collapsed roof. Descend the long staircase to take a look at the gorgeous icefalls formed around 2000 years ago. The Slovak Karst is also the place where you can find the longest gorge in Slovakia – the 3-kilometre-long Zádielská tiesňava. Formed by limestone cliffs towering up to 250 metres high, in some places it is only 10 metres wide. The canyon is the natural habitat for a number of rare animal and plant species, the biggest of which are the eagle and black stork. The Slovak Karst is undoubtedly a remarka-

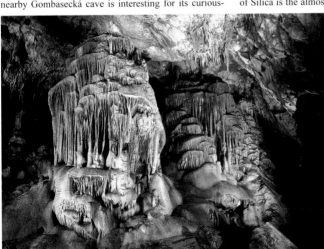

Domica is one of the most beautiful caves in Europe.

ble place with a great potential for further tourism development. Its natural beauty, its many way-marked trails, its ideal hiking and cycling, and abundance of castles, chateaux and unique medieval churches make it one of the most attractive parts of Slovakia.

The central square in Rožňava is dominated by a watchtower.

Rožňava

Situated in south-eastern Slovakia, Rožňava (population 20,000) is the capital of the historical Gemer region and a gateway to the Slovak Karst National Park. Begun as a miners' settlement in the 13th century, Rožňava became a free royal town in 1410 and enjoyed a century of great prosperity, profiting from its gold mining activities. The Turkish invasions which followed – the town was even burnt down by Ottoman soldiers- precipitated a long period of stagnation. Development came to an end – new houses were built only in a small ring around the central market square – and in the 16th century, due to the presence of the Turkish in-

Gemer

The historical region of Gemer in the south-eastern corner of Slovakia is noted for its thriving folk culture, natural beauty and precious Gothic churches.

vaders nearby, the mining industry went into a decline and disappeared altogether by the end of the next century. In 1776, the Empress Maria Theresa established the Rožňava Bishopric, which gave the municipality a new

impetus for development. The old town quarter of modern Rožňava is formed by a unique square-shaped central square with the late-Renaissance watchtower from 1643-54. Rožňava's present symbol was for a long time a part of the Town Hall, which was subsequently destroyed by fire. On the site of the burnt-out building, a Jesuit church was built in 1658-87 by, interestingly, the local Protestants. The square is flanked by pretty burgher houses, most of them with baroque and classical facades. Underneath the houses are openings to the galleries of the medieval mines, excavated right beneath the square. In the northern part of the square is the residence of the bishop, consisting of several older houses, and in the corner is the late-Baroque Franciscan church and monastery from the end of the 18th century. Rožňava's most important sacred building, the Episcopal Cathedral with a number of beautiful Gothic artefacts, is situated nearby. Completed in the 14th century, the church acquired new chapels following a massive reconstruction a hundred years later. With Rožňava becoming the centre of the diocese in 1776, this parish church was restored in the baroque style, its wooden tower being replaced by a baroque one and the church being promoted to cathedral status. One of the most precious artefacts in the cathedral is the late Gothic table painting ascribed to the school of Master

Rožňava's landmarks – the Episcopal Cathedral and Franciscan Church.

Pavol of Levoča. At the rear of the church are paintings depicting authentic scenes of the miners' work.

Štítnik

Begun as a miners' settlement in the 13th century, the next hundred years saw this interesting hamlet develop into a busy market town. Its irregular triangular-shaped square is surrounded by buildings with attractive facades that once housed local burghers and craftsmen.

The main point of interest in Štítnik, and the most precious sacred building in the whole Gemer region, is the Gothic Protestant Church with a massive tower, completed in the early 15th century. The most beautiful feature of the church is its intricate arches. The church was presented to the Protestants in the 16th century, who em-

Most of the interior of the church in Štítnik is covered by precious frescoes.

barked on a substantial reconstruction of the building, covering over the precious frescoes with sacred motifs from the 14th-16th centuries. The paintings, extending over an area of 200 square metres in all, were revealed

at the beginning of the 20th century. It must have been a challenging job, as in some places the frescoes were covered by up to three layers of paint. The interior of the church boasts a number of different artefacts and exudes an atmosphere of harmony and perfection.

Krásna Hôrka

Built on a steep conical hill near Rožňava, Krásna Hôrka Castle dominates the surrounding countryside. Begun in 1320, the castle, situated in a hilly region,

Krásna Hôrka Castle is situated on the top of a tall conical hill.

served in the first centuries of its existence as an important base in the wars against the Turks. In the middle of the 16th century it was rebuilt in the Renaissance style into a fortress and passed from the hands of the Bebek family to the prominent Andrássys, who made it into a magnificent residence. In 1817, the castle was struck by lightning and suffered great damage. For the next hun-

Since 1910 it has been a museum.

Mausoleum

The last owner of Krásna Hôrka Castle, Dionýz Andrássy, had an attractive rotunda-shaped Art Nouveau mausoleum built in 1903-04 in honour of his deceased wife, the Czech opera singer Francisca Hablawetz. It is one of the finest examples of the Art Nouveau style in Slovakia.

ous expeditions of the Andrássys to Africa and America, including mummies, elephant tusks and the shells of giant turtles. Another interesting feature is the cave-like entrance. The manor is situated in a large 80-hectare park, designed according to the tenets of Jean Jacques Rousseau's 'back to nature' philosophy by the renowned German landscape architect Heinrich Neblien. The fairy-tale arbours, waterfalls, lakes and exotic trees and plants give the surroundings of the palace a roman-

dred years, the building lay in ruins until it was reconstructed by Dionýz Andrassy, following the death of his wife, at the beginning of the 20th century. The castle was reopened in 1910 and has served as the museum of the Andrássy clan ever since. The exhibition of family memorabilia was later augmented by a collection of medieval weapons. Another attraction of the castle is the mummified body of Zsófia Serédyi, one of the castle's former owners.

By the road from the village to the Krásna Hôrka Castle is a mausoleum with the grave of the wife of Dionýz Andrássy, the Czech opera singer Francisca Hablawetz. A commoner, Hablowetz was never accepted by the Andrássys and could not be buried in the family shrine. The rotunda-shaped mausoleum, built in the 1903-04 by architect Berndl from Munich, is one of the most prized Art Nouveau buildings in Slovakia and the symbol of the eternal love between Andrássy and Hablowetz. Andrássy was also a dedicated collector of paintings and had a gallery in the Art Nouveau style built in the village below the castle in 1908-09, where he installed a collection of portraits from all over Hungary.

The unique park in Betliar is full of romantic arbours.

tic atmosphere. The brook that flows through the gardens is part of a sophisticated irrigation system. In 1977, the park, still faithful to its original 18th-century design, was added to the list of Historical Landscape Gardens of the World of the International Committee for Historical Gardens (ICOMOS-IFLA).

Park in Betliar

Travellers and collectors as they were, the Andrássys brought back a number of artefacts and trophies from their travels. They are now on display in the manor and the park.

Betliar

In the 18th century, the Andrássy family moved from Krásna Hôrka Castle to the nearby Betliar Manor. Formerly a Renaissance manor of the Bebek family, it underwent many reconstructions until it took on its present appearance in the 19th century. The palace, one of the best-preserved buildings of its kind in Slovakia, boasts a well-stocked library and trophies from numer-

Betliar is one of Slovakia's most beautiful and best-preserved manors.

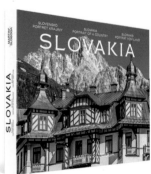